THE JOURNEY OF THE

Western Horse

The Journey of the Western Horse

From the Spanish Conquest to the Silver Screen

Les Sellnow

EP

ECLIPSE
PRESS

Lexington, Kentucky

Library of Congress Control Number: 2002114039

ISBN 1-58150-094-7

Printed in Hong Kong
First Edition: July 2003

Distributed to the trade by
National Book Network
4720-A Boston Way
Lanham, MD 20706
1.800.462.6420

a division of
Blood-Horse Publications
PUBLISHERS SINCE 1916

Contents

Contents

In The Beginning

1

The western horse is used for everything from herding cattle to carrying riders cross-country on relaxing trail rides. It is ridden in sophisticated dressage routines and soars over high fences in Grand Prix jumping.

This versatility didn't come about by accident. It is the product of thousands of years of evolution and development. Some of the development has been at the hands of nature and some through man's manipulation of genetics in selective breeding.

What is the "western horse"?

The western horse is an amalgamation of bloodlines that were fused to produce a rugged, utilitarian animal for early settlers of the United States. These horses varied in appearance almost as much as they varied in function. The lighter horses were used as riding animals and for racing, the heavier ones pulled plows over fields and Conestoga wagons across the continent.

Over time stallions with certain characteristics have been mated to mares with similar characteristics, further defining the breeds that epitomize the western horse. These are the Quarter Horse, Appaloosa, and Paint. The crossbred is also considered a western horse, though its variety of bloodlines might preclude it from being registered as one of the above breeds.

Scientific research has unearthed genetic knowledge that has turned breeding into a sophisticated science, often allowing the breeder to produce a specific type of horse for a particular discipline. Cutting horses, for example, have become shorter with sturdy legs for quick stops and turns through selective breeding.

Yet, as sophisticated as breeding practices have

The western horse is a versatile animal but best known as a cowboy's companion.

become, there are no guarantees. Sometimes traits believed to have been bred out of a particular bloodline will crop up through a recessive gene that had to await the correct linkup to make its presence felt.

The horse's genetic code has developed through millions of years. Much of the early development occurred in North America, South America, Asia, and later in Europe, where horses roamed in vast numbers. Of course, the very early equines were far different from today's horses. Scientists estimate that the remote ancestor of the horse was no larger than a fox, with four toes on the front feet and three toes on the back feet. They eventually evolved into fleet three-toed creatures about the size of sheep.

Later, the three toes gave way to a hoof. Early horses began to vary in type and size. Among the

The Quarter Horse has evolved from its prehistoric ancestors to one of the world's most popular and versatile breeds.

smaller European breeds, for example, was the Shetland Pony, which likely descended from the small, shaggy wild stock of northern Europe. The largest of the European horses, to which today's draft stock traces its lineage, appears to have descended primarily from the heavyset wild horses of Flanders.

The European horses, as well as those found in Asia, are believed to have sprung from horses that at one time inhabited North America and South America. Scientists believe the American horses, dating back some fifty million years, crossed the Bering Strait on a land bridge that once connected Alaska and Siberia. Then, a strange thing happened: All of the horses in North America and South America perished. Scientists aren't sure just when this occurred but estimate it was between ten thousand and twenty-five thousand years ago. Whatever the time frame, the fact remains that when Europeans discovered America, no horses were found. Theories abound, but no one can be certain what happened. One plausible explanation is that a disease, perhaps insect-borne, swept the equine populations in the Americas, wiping them out. It was not until Columbus arrived in the Americas that horses would once again set foot in the Western Hemisphere.

Just when the horse was domesticated is also open to debate. A bone heap found in the Rhone Valley of southern France contained various remains of one hundred thousand horses consumed by inhabitants.

To Stone Age hunters, the horse was just another edible wild animal stalked on foot, not a fleet beast for riding.

Of course, the horse was also prey for large flesh-eating predators, such as lions, tigers, and wolves, and remains so today wherever it exists in the wild. Because it is a prey animal, the horse's greatest weapon against predators has always been flight. The animal that could outrun pursuers survived and produced others of its kind. The slow-of-foot horse was caught and eaten, and its genes weren't passed on.

Later, man would take advantage of the horse's speed by, ironically, using the horse to catch prey. Indian hunters on horseback could outrun buffalo and kill them with arrows, lances, or firearms. The horse's speed and agility also made it well suited for the battlefield. Horses may have initially been domesticated for that purpose.

About the seventh century B.C., the Scythians, who were fierce warriors with long, flowing hair and beards, began using horses for battle. These nomads of central Asia would charge their enemies at full gallop as they fired arrows, a method later used by Native Americans.

The Scythians, who also used horses as draft animals and for cross-country riding, became accomplished horsemen, and some historians credit them with inventing the bridle and saddle.

As the Scythians' herds grew, the nomads looked for greener pastures. They migrated westward, raiding and pillaging as they went, until they reached the Ukraine steppe with its mighty sea of grass. This must have seemed like heaven because here they could graze their herds of horses, cattle, and sheep without worry about there being enough forage.

By the third century A.D., the Scythians had disappeared. Left behind to tell their story were lavish tombs outfitted for the next world, sometimes complete with horses and grooms.

Interestingly, the Egyptians, the most advanced civilization of the day, are believed to have domesticated and used the donkey years before they used the horse, which was introduced in 1680 B.C. during the dynasty of the Shepherd Kings, who came to Egypt from Asia.

The Egyptians helped to develop the chariot, which became one of their favorite means of waging war, as well as a mode of transportation.

Most people familiar with the Old Testament recall how Egyptian soldiers in chariots were sent after escaping Israelites being led by Moses from Egypt toward the Promised Land about 1500 B.C. The biblical account tells us that the Red Sea parted until the Israelites reached the other side, and when the Egyptian charioteers sought to follow, the waters closed and rolled over them, sending horses and soldiers to a watery grave.

The Greeks also used horse-drawn chariots to wage war, as evidenced in their siege of Troy, which ended about 1184 B.C. From Greece, the horse made its way to Rome and then to other parts of Europe. Many Romans became master horsemen, as both drivers and riders. They, too, used chariots in war as well as in the sport of racing, but many of their troops were mounted when they went into battle.

While the Arabian horse is credited with influencing all of the known light-boned horse breeds, the Arabs themselves did not have an appreciable number of horses until the time of Mohammed, some six hundred years after the birth of Christ.

Thus, rather than providing the foundation for the modern horse, the Arabs were relative latecomers on the equine scene. Once they arrived, however, they quickly became expert horsemen and knowledgeable breeders. The Arabs maintained elaborate pedigrees on their horses, and through selective breeding, they developed a small but hardy horse with incredible stamina. It also possessed great beauty.

Stories are told of how Bedouin raiders — fierce nomadic tribesmen who inhabit the deserts of Arabia — would ride camels and lead their war horses toward an enemy camp. Once the Bedouins were within striking distance, the camels were sent back and the nomadic attackers would mount their fleet horses — almost always mares because a stallion might whinny and give away their position — and charge. After the battle, they would flee on their tough little horses, often traveling across the desert sands for hours at full speed without stops for food or water.

Although the Bedouins recognized the value of a good stallion in their breeding program, they especially prized their elite war mares and broodmares. Legend has it that the most valuable mare would often spend nights in its owner's tent to protect it against theft or from the elements.

These tough animals that carried the Bedouins over the desert sands are descendants of the now-extinct wild horses of the Asiatic deserts.

Eventually horses were imported to Spain and from there to the Americas. There is much debate about what type of horses the Spaniards brought to this country because they didn't specify them by breed, only by color and personality. Some researchers hold that the first imports were Arabians; while others believe they most likely were Barbs (more heavily boned and not quite so pretty), Andalusians, or, perhaps, a mixture of the above. The only certainty is that these first imports appear to have been light horses, which means they likely carried at least some Arabian, Barb, or Turk blood.

Most accounts indicate that the horses were small and light but very sturdy. They had to be sturdy. When the Spaniards went into battle, they fitted the horses with steel breastplates and clothed themselves in steel armor. All of that equipment, plus the rider, would result in a heavy burden for the horse.

Another indication these horses were not tall was recorded during Fernando de Soto's invasion of what is now Florida. At one point, de Soto put one of the native chieftains on a horse and led it about. The man was so tall that his feet touched the ground.

It is unlikely there were men in Florida at that time who were so tall their feet would reach the ground when astride a fifteen-hand horse. It is more likely that the man was indeed tall and that the horse on which he rode was indeed short. The horses of the Spanish invaders were also described as having short backs, giving further rise to the speculation of a strong Arabian influence.

Christopher Columbus reintroduced the horse to this continent when he discovered the Americas in 1492. He recorded that on board the ships that landed in the West Indies were six mares, along with four jackasses, two female donkeys, four bull calves, two heifers, one hundred sheep and goats, eighty boars, and twenty sows. On his second voyage Columbus brought more horses, and during ensuing years almost every Spanish ship that sailed to the New World carried horses. While gold and other treasures, such as spices, seemed to motivate Spanish exploration, Columbus, for one, recognized that newly established settlements would need an economy based on something more sustainable — like cattle ranching and farming.

With so many horses being shipped to the New World to meet the growing need, Spain experienced a shortage. As a result, the king temporarily banned the shipment of horses to the New World.

The voyage could not have been easy on the horses. The trip took weeks and sometimes included a short layover at the Spanish-controlled Canary Islands. The horses were allowed little movement. For the most part, they were tied out in the open on the wooden deck of the ship. This meant that those not valuable enough to be sheltered by an overhang stood in the hot sun, wind, and rain. When the seas were abnormally rough, slings might have been used to help the horses maintain balance.

Then there were the calms. Those were the days when the wind didn't blow hard enough to fill the sails, and the ship just floated there on glassy seas. When water supplies ran low, the horses were the first to be deprived and many died of thirst. The dead were unceremoniously pitched overboard. These flat stretches became known as the "horse latitudes." Despite the hardships, many horses survived to become the nucleus of the vast herds that soon roamed the Americas.

Explorer Hernando Cortez landed the first horses on the North American mainland. On March 13, 1519, near what is now Vera Cruz, Mexico, Cortez unloaded sixteen horses. Later, colleague Pedro de Alvarado brought another twenty horses and one hundred and fifty men. Not exactly a monstrous cavalry.

The horses that Cortez landed in Mexico included five mares and eleven stallions, as the Spanish gelded few horses in those days. Eight were bay or sorrel; two brown; three gray; one black; and two were spotted. While we know about their color and sex from the explorers' written reports, we know very little about the horses' conformation and bloodlines.

The native inhabitants (Aztecs) that Cortez encountered had never before seen a horse. Nor, for that matter, had they seen light-skinned Spaniards. The natives were in awe. In the beginning, the Aztecs thought that man and horse were one and that the fearsome creature was some sort of god. The Spaniards would play on those fears, seeking to convince the natives that the horses were flesh eaters to be feared and might attack at the least provocation.

A story is told that at one point Cortez was parlaying for peace with a group of Aztecs. The scene threatened to become ugly because the natives were unwilling to yield to his demands. Cortez ordered a stallion be brought near the negotiating site where a mare was tied. Cortez then ordered the mare removed. The stallion, seeing the mare moving away from him, began to prance, whinny, and paw the ground.

Cortez had his men lead the stallion away. He told the Aztecs that the stallion had been instructed not to harm them if they were in favor of peace. It seems the frightened natives quickly agreed to the terms.

Their fear dissipated after seeing horses killed in battle. A chief had the head of one removed and carried from village to village to let the people know that the horse was mortal.

Though the natives vastly outnumbered the Spaniards, they could not overcome the mounted contingent.

In 1528 the first horses arrived on what was to become the United States of America. They landed in what is now Florida, with an expedition under the command of Pánfilo de Narváez. Before the expedition ever arrived in Florida, however, forty-two of the eighty animals died during the voyage from Spain.

Many members of the crew also perished. One of the few men to survive the expedition, Alvar Nuñez Cabeza de Vaca, went on to explore the coast of Texas and areas farther west. Unfortunately, all of the horses that survived the voyage came to a rather sorry end. Natives killed many of them in attacks, and the soldiers ate those that remained, using their skins to help make boats to explore the shoreline.

A much larger group of horses, between two hundred and fifty and three hundred, arrived about ten years later with an expedition led by Fernando de Soto.

De Soto wasn't exactly virtuous. He won fame and honor from his peers and rulers by helping to subjugate Peru. He was authorized by his government to "conquer, pacify and populate" Florida. He had carte blanche to do as he saw fit in overpowering inhabitants and taking what he so desired. De Soto's popularity in Spain helped the thirty-seven-year-old attract men of similar age and aristocratic breeding to join his quest to the New World. He sailed from Spain with ten ships and some six hundred young men.

De Soto went first to Cuba where he stayed about a year, gathering supplies and the best horses for his expedition through Florida and beyond. He sailed from Havana to present-day Tampa Bay in May 1539. Twenty horses died during the nineteen-day voyage.

Disaster plagued the expedition from the beginning. A native's arrow killed one of the first horses to step on shore. From there things only worsened. As de Soto stubbornly pushed north looking for gold and other treasures, he engaged the Native Americans in battles, causing him to constantly lose men and horses.

In one battle near present-day Mobile, Alabama, at least twelve horses were killed and seventy-plus wounded.

True to the European traditions of the time, the invading army lived off the land, plundering and taking what it wanted from the inhabitants. After two years of wandering and battling, the expedition arrived at the Mississippi River. The Spaniards and their horses were in sad shape, but still de Soto would not turn back. A year later and three years after the expedition began, de Soto died of a fever. By this time, only forty of the original horses were still alive. Yet another year would go by before the Spaniards, minus de Soto's leadership, decided they'd had enough. They used logs to build boats to carry themselves down the Mississippi to the Gulf of Mexico. By then only twenty-two horses remained.

Ultimately, the natives would kill these horses, though romanticized accounts tell of some horses escaping and linking up with other escapees in the West. Most historians agree that none of de Soto's horses survived. When the Spaniards finally boarded their boats for home, only five horses remained, and they were set free. The natives promptly killed them.

Explorer Francisco Vásquez de Coronado led a trip in 1540 that also had tragic consequences for his horses. Again, greed for treasure and conquest prompted the journey. Coronado began in Mexico and worked his way north, seeking the fabled but non-existent "Seven Cities of Gold." The expedition included between 1,200 and 1,500 horses and pack mules. The group traveled through northern Mexico and into what is now Arizona. They found no gold, only small villages of Native Americans.

There were battles, but, again, the horses made the difference. These Native Americans, too, had never seen horses and were terrified of them. Disappointed at not finding the "Seven Cities of Gold" where they were reported to be, Coronado sent groups of soldiers exploring the surrounding countryside. One expedition traversed the Colorado Plateau and crossed the Painted Desert. Another expedition, guided by Hopi Indians, marched for twenty days and came to the edge of the Grand Canyon. But, still there was no gold.

Coronado moved toward the Rio Grande for winter quarters, continuing to live off native inhabitants. One village's inhabitants attacked Coronado and his men as they approached. The Spaniards retaliated by destroying twelve villages and driving occupants into the Sangre de Cristo Mountains.

When spring came, Coronado pushed farther north in his search for gold and silver. His passion for fortune and fame was fired to a fever pitch when he came upon a Native American who told about his homeland far to the north where gold and silver were plentiful. Coronado set off with a small group, traveling across what has come to be known as the Texas Panhandle and trekking on to the great open grasslands of Kansas.

There was no gold, and there was no silver on the banks of the Arkansas River, only another village.

During this side trip, the main body of the expedition ran into disaster. The Spaniards were in western Mexico when a vicious hailstorm hit. Nearly all of the horses and mules broke free and ran off.

Coronado returned to find the main expedition in disarray with nearly all of the horses and mules missing. The expedition straggled back to Mexico. Coronado lived out his life in obscurity.

What about the horses that escaped?

Do the wild horse herds of later years trace back to those that escaped and ran off during the hailstorm? Were these the horses captured by Native Americans and turned into hunting and war mounts?

Probably not, though some may have survived. Reportedly, only a few of the horses taken on the expedition were mares. It is also likely that predators, animal and human, hunted down many of the escapees. But, the fact remains that the Native Americans did acquire horses and horses did change their way of life. Those horses, for the most part, came into the possession of Native Americans when the Pueblo Indians revolted against their Spanish masters and temporarily drove them out.

The Western Horse and the Native American

2

Meaningful progress or historic change usually occurs over hundreds or even thousands of years, but there are exceptions.

One occurred when Native Americans, who traveled by foot or canoe, discovered the horse.

The horse completely changed certain Native American cultures. Semi-nomadic tribes became complete nomads and, in some instances, tribes that farmed abandoned that way of life. They, too, became at least semi-nomadic.

The horse changed some Native American tribes from a farming lifestyle to a nomadic way of life.

Chief Medicine Owl

Native Americans in the West procured their first substantial number of horses in 1680 following a Pueblo uprising in a remote corner of the Southwest now known as New Mexico.

From the time Cortez landed in Mexico in 1519, a steady trickle of people, and horses, continued to arrive in the New World from Spain, but it was not a flood of newcomers. By 1629, more than one hundred years after Cortez, there were still fewer than one thousand Spanish-speaking people in all of Mexico.

Spanish soldier-settlers developed farms and ranches along the Rio Grande, exacting labor from the native Pueblo Indians as though they were serfs or slaves. Things were done that way in Spain, and the Spaniards merely imposed their feudal agricultural system on the New World. The wealthy and powerful owned the land. The weak, from a military point of view, and the poor tilled the soil and tended the herds and flocks.

New Mexico officially became a royal colony in 1595; its rulers headquartered in Santa Fe, a village on a tributary of the Rio Grande.

In the beginning, Roman Catholic priests made Santa Fe their headquarters and traveled forth to convert the Native American population to Christianity.

Later, a group of thirty Franciscan friars, escorted by a small contingent of soldiers, sailed from Spain to Mexico. The friars, filled with religious zeal, were determined to replace what they considered the pagan practices of Native Americans with Christian worship. The Franciscans made their way to New Mexico and spread throughout the territory, preaching the Word and building churches.

Fearing the Spanish, many of the Pueblos pretended to be converts while in private they practiced their own religion.

The Spanish, recognizing how the horse had enabled them to dominate the Native Americans in Mexico, refused to allow the Pueblos to own hors-

Horses enabled Native Americans to hunt buffalo more effectively.

es. This, of course, did not prevent some enterprising natives from stealing the animals from their conquerors.

But no matter what the Native Americans did to thwart the invaders, nothing could protect them from the diseases the Spaniards brought. With no immunity, the Native Americans contracted maladies such as smallpox, diphtheria, measles, and tuberculosis. Because their bodies could not fight off the diseases, they died by the hundreds and even thousands. Some twenty thousand natives died in 1638 alone and in 1640 another epidemic wiped out another ten thousand.

Nature exacerbated these already unpleasant conditions. Beginning in 1660, a drought seared the land and crops. Raids by the Apache and Navajo, two tribes that had not been subjugated by the Spanish, added to the Pueblos' plight.

Tribal leaders and medicine men were chafing under the religious intolerance imposed by the Spanish as well as the serfdom that had turned many of the natives into virtual slaves. The drought convinced them their gods were demonstrating unhappiness with them for allowing the Spanish to remain in their land.

Secretly, under the leadership of a holy man named Popé, the Pueblos plotted an uprising. On August 10, 1680, in villages across northern New Mexico, the Pueblos rose up and overthrew their priests and friars, killing many of them and razing the churches.

Settlers, soldiers, and friars alike fled to Santa Fe. Twenty-five hundred Pueblos quickly surrounded the town. The siege continued for some days, but the remaining Spaniards fought their way out and fled south toward El Paso. The rebellious natives likely could have killed them as they fled, but the rebels, happy to be free of Spanish rule and oppression, allowed the survivors to escape.

When the Spanish fled, they left behind thousands of animals. The Pueblos did not consider the horses and cattle a major windfall. They preferred raising sheep, which were not as difficult to maintain and did not require as much forage and range as horses and cattle.

While these were not the Pueblos' first horses, they were the first to change hands from Spaniard to native in appreciable numbers.

Because the Pueblos preferred sheep to horses and cattle, they began trading the Spanish horses to the Apaches and Navajos, who, in turn, began trading them to tribes farther north. Before 1680 ended, horses had already made their way to the Plains tribes of Texas. Ten years later, horses had reached the Kiowa and Comanche tribes in what is now Colorado.

By the 1800s horses were spreading to the tribes of the northern Plains via two main routes. On one route, horse traders traveled from the Spanish settlements and Native American tribes of New Mexico and Texas to the Black Hills of South Dakota, and from there, east and northeast to the Arikara, Hidatsa, and Mandan villages on the Missouri River.

The second route led from the upper Yellowstone River east to the Hidatsa and Mandan villages, turning them into horse-trading centers. Tribes from all directions traveled to the villages to trade for horses and mules.

The Cheyenne were a perfect example of how the horse could completely alter a tribe's existence.

Before the Cheyenne acquired horses, they had been a sedentary people, living along the banks of streams in Minnesota and planting and tending crops of corn, beans, and squash, among other vegetables. The Lakota, however, began pushing the Cheyenne west. At the beginning of the eighteenth century the Cheyenne wound up in what is now South Dakota, where they found horses.

Now with the horse, a Cheyenne warrior could run down and kill buffalo with relative ease. No longer did the Cheyenne have to stalk their prey or stampede them over cliffs. The horse turned the Native American into a more effective hunter, enabling him to provide food and clothing when buffalo were present.

The Cheyenne ceased farming and became

nomads, following the buffalo as the great herds migrated across the vast seas of grass that were the Great Plains. However, the arrival of the horse had also changed the lifestyle of other tribes, bringing about congestion, a problem most people think of as occurring today in big cities and not on the Great Plains in the 1800s.

The Great Plains had been sparsely populated because the vast distances and lack of water discouraged foot travel. This changed with the arrival of the horse. As many as thirty tribes now traveled across the Plains in their quest for buffalo. Encounters with other travelers, rare before the horse, now were frequent and not always peaceable. Horses enabled riders to better wield their weapons. Carrying a lance or bow and arrow, a warrior on horseback was much more effective than one on foot.

Horses became the measure of a warrior's stature within the tribe. Honored was the man who owned a horse that was fleet and brave when racing through a herd of buffalo or carrying a rider into battle. Because they brought the owner great esteem, such horses were virtually priceless.

Horses also became, in a manner of speaking, the coin of the realm. They were used in bartering everything from weapons to wives. A warrior's financial worth was equated with the number of horses he owned. Warriors could own up to several hundred horses, creating a large herd for their tribe.

Maintaining the herd contributed to the Native Americans' nomadic way of life. A tribe would move into an area, set up camp, and remain until the horses exhausted the grass supply. The availability of grass and water was basic in choosing each new location for their tepee village.

As warriors became more familiar with the horse, they became adept rid-

ers. Perhaps the most adept were the Comanche. Comanche warriors learned to guide their hunting and war horses with leg pressure. They also could cling to the side of a horse when it was running at full speed. Using its body as a shield, warriors fired arrows from beneath its neck.

A sling of hair rope, with both ends braided into the horse's mane, helped warriors maintain that precarious position. The rider hooked an elbow into this sling while digging a heel into the horse's back.

Native Americans' war horses often doubled as buffalo-running horses. The buffalo runner was trained to race along the animal's right side. The hunter would drop the reins and use both hands to fire arrows into the buffalo. Later the Native American hunters would use the same process with guns. If the hunter missed with an arrow or a rifle, the horse was trained to remain alongside the buffalo while the rider reloaded or prepared another arrow.

Both the warpath and the hunt were fraught with danger for the horse. When being ridden into battle, the horse was vulnerable to arrows, bullets, or lances. When being ridden after buffalo, a stumble could

The horse was a measure of a warrior's stature.

mean instant death by trampling for both horse and rider. There was also the added danger that a wounded buffalo would stop fleeing and attack the horse that was tormenting it. With sharp horns and a powerful thrust, a buffalo could, in a second, inflict a painful and often fatal wound to the horse's midsection.

The Native American of the Plains accepted these dangers as part of life, but he also learned to treat a wounded or injured horse. George Bird Grinnell, who first visited a Cheyenne camp in 1890, later wrote two volumes titled *The Cheyenne Indians, History and Society*. We are indebted to him for information concerning the first Native American veterinarians. They were called horse doctors, but also plied their trade on humans. There was more mysticism than veterinary science in their approach perhaps, but their very existence indicates concern about equine welfare.

In a Cheyenne horse doctor's lodge, Grinnell wrote, family members had to follow rigid protocol. For example, when the woman of the family rose in the morning, she had to strike the lodge pole four times before making any noise. If the marrow bone of an animal were broken in the lodge, one of the family's horses would supposedly break one of its legs.

All members of the horse doctor's family were expected to hang up equipment, such as reatas or lariats, bridles, and whips, in the lodge. The items would be hung on a forked stick at the head of the bed. To leave any of the equipment on the ground, they believed, would result in the offender being thrown from his horse and injured.

When the Cheyenne sent out a large war party, several horse doctors would usually go as well. Before battle, one of the horse doctors would walk back and forth over the horses' tracks, singing and chanting, seeking to exercise his power so that none of the horses would be hurt.

The same ceremony was often conducted prior to a buffalo hunt.

Medicine, of course, also had to be administered according to ritual. The doctor would hold the medicine bag in his left hand and use his right hand to put a pinch of the medicine inside the horse's mouth. Then, with the same hand, he would put a pinch into his own mouth and blow it against the horse's body just behind the right shoulder. Next, he would rub his hand over where he had blown the medicine. He did the same to the horse's right flank.

Switching sides and hands, he followed the same procedure on the left. The ritual also involved rubbing the medicine on the horse's head from the nostrils to over the ears.

When the process was finished, the horse was turned loose. If the horse rolled shortly after being freed, the medicine was declared good and the horse, they believed, would be cured. However, if the horse did not roll, this indicated the treatment had failed.

The horse doctors used two kinds of medicine, each from a different plant, Grinnell wrote. He did not identify the plants. One was carried in a bag tied with plaited hair from the horse's tail, the other in a bag tied with deerskin. Both medications, he said, were used to revive and strengthen a horse when it was tired. For illness, rather than injuries or wounds, the horse medicine was dissolved in its drinking water. No horse doctor would eat horseflesh, and no horse doctor would ever shoot a horse, wild or tame.

The Cheyenne horse doctors, some of whom were women, normally did not set a price for their services. They were paid with a horse, sometimes a blanket, arrows, robes, or maybe even a saddle.

Many Native American tribes produced excellent horsemen and women. Captain R.B. Marcy, a cavalryman who was part of an 1849 expedition to the Red River, said that during a visit to a Comanche camp he saw two young women, armed only with lassos, ride after a herd of antelope. When the antelope sped off, the women raced after them and each roped one on the first try.

Young Native American boys learned to ride almost from infancy. It was their job to day-herd the horses, and they likely spent most of that time playing games on horseback and, thus, perfecting their riding skills at an early age. They learned to pick up small objects from the ground while galloping at full speed. They even learned to swing under the belly of a running horse, aided by the sling or rawhide rope braided into the mane. All of these activities helped make them fierce warriors and skilled hunters from horseback.

In a sense, these talented riders became one with the horse. In fact, many of them spent so much time on horseback that, according to George Catlin, an artist and writer who lived with various Native American tribes from 1832 through 1839, the Comanches were actually rather clumsy on the ground.

Most Native Americans rode bareback, but when saddles were used, they were of poor quality, usually a skin pad stuffed with hair or a wooden frame modeled after what they had seen the Spaniards use. In some cases, the wooden frames were poorly lined and didn't fit the horse's back very well. As a result, frequently ridden horses usually developed sore backs.

Meriwether Lewis of the Lewis and Clark expedition reported seeing some sore-backed horses accompanying the Native Americans they encountered. However, he reported, the sores and abrasions weren't so serious that the horses couldn't be ridden. The wounds were often covered with a rag or animal skin to ward off flies and magpies, which would land on the horses and pick at exposed flesh.

The Native Americans took care of their horses, and good ones were highly valued and rarely for sale. Captain Marcy wrote about offering a Comanche chief a large sum for his celebrated horse and being turned down because the horse was one of the tribe's fleetest. The chief said the horse assured success in the buffalo hunt, so to sell him at any price would be very foolish and calamitous to the tribe.

The Cheyenne earned a deserved reputation as outstanding horsemen.

Besides, he told Marcy, he loved the horse very much.

Horses owned by the Native Americans of the western Plains had to be hardy, especially in the winter, when snow covered the ground. During the summer, forage was everywhere, but during the winter it could be pretty slim pickings. When possible, the horses would dig through snow and ice with their hooves to get at the cured grass beneath. When the snow was too deep or the ground covered with ice, the horses turned to the bark of trees along river valleys for sustenance.

During the first winter of their expedition, Lewis, Clark, and their accompanying soldiers and civilians stayed with the Mandan tribe of North Dakota. They reported that during the winter, the Mandans offered bran mash to some of their hungry horses. The animals, they said, turned away from it, preferring cottonwood bark. Some select Mandan horses were taken into lodges at night and hand fed dried grass, bark, or small tree branches, while others were freed to fend for themselves.

If the snow and ice thawed and grass showed up in the distance, individuals and groups of horses probably wandered off and did not return. And, because few of the Indian horses were gelded, the wild herds propagated rapidly.

Accounts show that the northern tribes of the Great Plains had more high-quality horses than the southern tribes. The difference had more to do with a higher quality of grass in the north than with breeding.

Early on, tribes in need of horses would peacefully exchange goods and supplies for horses from tribes with a more plentiful supply. However, as the number of horses increased and conflicts escalated between groups and tribes, bartering took a back seat to thievery.

Stealing horses became a way of life, almost a sacred calling, for some Plains tribes of the West. Successful horse thieves were as celebrated for their feats as were warriors who counted coup — actually reaching out and touching an enemy — in battle or excelled in killing buffalo.

Grinnell wrote that the Cheyenne, whom he came to know and respect, sometimes went to war solely to acquire more horses. They had no interest in taking scalps or counting coup, only in capturing their enemies' horses.

Grinnell wrote about a Cheyenne named Big Foot who was riding a very fast horse during a war party foray. When he saw one of his enemies mounted on a fine-looking horse, he set off in pursuit. Big Foot's horse overtook that of his adversary. Instead of killing the other warrior, however, he roped him, dragged him from the horse, and then let the man go. Big Foot caught the horse his enemy had ridden and returned to camp.

Another time, Big Foot and two fellow warriors came upon a lone Ute horseman. The Ute was shot from the saddle, and Big Foot's two companions raced toward the downed man, each wanting to be the first to count coup. Big Foot ignored them and, instead, raced after and captured the Ute's horse.

Most horse thieves would usually slip into a village in the dark of night and free tethered or corralled horses. The thieves would then drive the horses out at full speed, gambling that surprise, confusion, and lack of horses with which to pursue them would ensure their successful escape.

To prevent such thefts, some warriors slept with their best war horse or buffalo runner tethered to their wrist or to an object inside the tent.

The warriors' horses were usually small, wiry, and exceedingly tough, with long manes and flowing tails that often touched the ground, according to George Catlin, a writer and artist fascinated with Native American life. He visited tribes ranging from the Comanches in the Southwest to the Mandans in North Dakota.

He also reported the horses he encountered varied in color, including some that were "milk-white, some jet black—others were sorrel, and bay, and cream colour—many were of an iron grey; and others were pied, containing a variety of colours on the same animal."

Was selective breeding employed or did the Native American operate on "luck of the draw" by allowing stallions and mares to intermingle in the herd? Little is known about this, other than with the Nez Perce, a Pacific Southwest tribe, which used selective breeding to produce the Appaloosa horse. We do know the Plains Indians thought racing to be great sport. If a warrior owned a fleet-footed mare and knew of a fast stallion, he would most likely seek to mate the two, so some form of selective breeding probably did take place.

By the time Catlin was visiting tribes in the 1830s, horses were abundant in the West. Many of them ran wild in herds so large that they almost rivaled buffalo in number. Eventually, that would change and once again the horse would become a hunted animal.

Wild Horses

3

Travelers crossing the Great Plains in the early to mid-1800s told of seeing buffalo herds so large that it might take more than a day and night for the migrating animals to pass.

The travelers also encountered enough horse herds to make them question whether horses had overtaken buffalo as the most populous animals on the prairie. Though they hadn't, the rise in the number of horses was still remarkable considering the animals had been re-introduced a few at a time only three hundred years earlier. It is estimated that in the early 1800s, between two million and three million wild horses roamed western rangeland.

Of course, these weren't true "wild" horses. They

Wild horses rivaled the buffalo in number during part of the nineteenth century.

were feral horses, meaning they descended from domestic animals. However, for the sake of this discussion we will call them wild horses because they roamed in the wild.

That neither the Spaniards nor the Native Americans favored gelding stallions spurred propagation. Both believed that gelding a horse reduced its power, energy, and spirit. Many of the stallions and mares from Native American bands and Spanish ranches escaped into the wild and reproduced freely on the open, wind-swept plains.

While traveling with a troop of U.S. cavalry through the Southwest on his way to a Comanche village in the 1800s, writer/artist George Catlin encountered herds of wild horses and captured their spirit both in words and with sketches.

"The tract of country over which we passed, between the False Washita (river) and this place," he wrote in *Letters and Notes on the North American Indians*, "is stocked, not only with buffaloes, but with numerous bands of wild horses, many of which we saw every day. There is no other animal on the prairies so wild and so sagacious as the horse; and none so difficult to come up with. So remarkably keen is their eye that they will generally run 'at the sight,' when they are a mile distant; and when in motion, will seldom stop short of three or four miles.

"I made many attempts to approach them by stealth, when they were grazing and playing gambol, without ever having been more than once able to succeed."

The one time he succeeded proved fatal to one of the wild horses. Catlin sneaked through a ravine until he was in gunshot range of a band. "Their manes were very profuse, and hanging in the wildest confusion over their necks and faces," he wrote, "and their long tails swept the ground."

First Catlin sketched the wild ones. When he finished, he and a friend decided to find out if they could "crease" one as they had heard described by wild horse hunters. That meant that they would nick the horse at the withers with a bullet to stun it, then hobble and capture it.

The two men leveled their rifles and fired. The horse dropped to the ground. They raced toward it, remembering as they ran that they did not have hobbles or a halter.

It didn't matter because when they got to the horse, they "had the still greater mortification, and even anguish, to find that one of our shots had broken the poor creature's neck, and that he was quite dead."

While an expert shot with a good rifle could capture a wild horse by "creasing," it was not standard procedure. Either roping wild horses or running them into makeshift corrals worked much better.

The Native Americans were among the first to capture wild horses, which later came to be called mustangs. (Mustang is a corruption of mesteño, the word the Spanish used for wild horses. The term for their pursuers became mustangers.) The warriors relied heavily on the lasso to capture wild horses, a practice they learned from the Spaniards. The Native Americans used lassos made of braided or twisted rawhide. The lassos ranged in length from thirty to forty-five feet.

Sometimes the warrior would pursue a wild horse with the fleetest mount he had. Other times, two or three warriors would team up to do the chasing. One would keep the wild horse running until his own mount tired, and then another warrior would take up the chase. This relay would go on until the wild horse became exhausted and could be roped with ease.

Once the loop settled around the wild horse's neck, the warrior would apply pressure. When the wild horse was "choked down," the warrior quickly dismounted and put hobbles on its front feet and a rope around its lower jaw. The warrior would loosen the lasso, and when the horse regained oxygen and strength, it was allowed to get to its feet. Then, the fight was on. The horse, though hobbled and restrained with the rope around its lower jaw, normally fought like the wild thing it was to get free.

The warrior would fight the animal until it was totally exhausted again. Once the horse gave up, the warrior removed the hobbles, sometimes leaping on the horse's back and riding off.

Catlin, who saw horses frequently caught this way, thought the horses caught by warriors working alone were inferior. The smart ones and the fast ones, he opined, either slipped away long before the warrior entered chasing range or else they had the speed to outrun their pursuer. He very well could be correct, but undoubtedly the approach provided the warriors with the excitement of a pell-mell chase, often over rocky and uneven ground.

The small, wiry wild horses were well suited to their terrain.

Catlin gave this description of the wild horses he observed:

"The wild horse of these regions is a small, but very powerful animal; with an exceedingly prominent eye, sharp nose, high nostril, small feet and delicate leg; and undoubtedly, have sprung from a stock introduced by the Spaniards, at the time of the invasion of Mexico; which having strayed off upon the prairies, have run wild, and stocked the plains from the Mexican border to Lake Winnipeg, two or three thousand miles to the north."

Though the wild horses weren't particularly large, they seem to have been more than an even match for predators such as wolves, mountain lions, and bears.

Though the Native Americans of the Plains regularly chased and caught wild horses, they did not impact the burgeoning population. The numbers of horses multiplied until hundreds of thousands roamed the prairies.

When Zebulon Pike led his expedition to Mexico in 1806, an advance guard of horsemen was needed to drive bands of wild horses out of the way. If that was not done, the travelers discovered, wild stallions would run off their domestic horses.

C.A. Murray, an Englishman who traveled across America between 1834 and 1836, described a wild horse stampede that occurred while he visited a Native American camp.

After tying the horses for the night, he said he thought he heard distant thunder.

"As it (the thunder) approached, it became mixed with the howling of all the dogs in the encampment, and with the shouts and yells of the Indians; in coming nearer, it rose high above those accompaniments, and resembled the lashing of a heavy surf

Wild horses of the 1800s were frequently described as small but sturdy.

upon a beach; on and on it rolled toward us, and partly from my own hearing, partly from the hurried words and actions of the tenants of our lodge, I gathered it must be the fierce and uncontrollable gallop of thousands of panic-stricken horses: as this living torrent drew nigh, I sprang to the front of the tent, seized my favorite riding mare, and in addition to the hobbles which confined her, twisted the long lariett (sic) round her forelegs, then led her immediately in front of the fire, hoping that the excited and maddened flood of horses would divide and pass on each side of it.

"As the galloping mass drew nigh, our horses began to snort, prick up their ears, then to tremble; and when it burst upon us, they became completely ungovernable from terror; all broke loose and joined their affrighted companions, except my mare which struggled with the fury of a wild beast, and I only retained her by using all my strength, and at last throwing her on her side. On went the maddened troop, trampling, in their headlong speed, over skins, dried meat, etc., and throwing down some of the smaller tents. They were soon lost in the darkness of the night, and in the wilds of the prairie…"

The 1830s marked the zenith of the wild horse herds. They were everywhere on the Great Plains and even inhabited some of the mountainous areas. They competed with the buffalo for grass and for what sometimes were scant supplies of water, especially during drought years. That all changed as settlers and ranchers headed west, and the change was quick and violent.

Texas was home to the country's first ranches, though it was part of Mexico at the time. Settlers migrated there in quest of free land and a new start when Mexico opened its borders to Americans in 1820. Many settlers turned to raising cattle.

As Americans migrated westward, they set their sights on California and Oregon. However, they noticed along the way that the lush grass of the Great Plains would make excellent feed for cattle.

A number of the homesteaders returned from the West Coast and established ranches on the Plains. To these ranchers and other ranchers who had traveled far to start anew, the wild horses and buffalo were competition for precious grass and water needed by their cattle. Wild stallions, these ranchers soon discovered, presented yet another problem. They were proficient at getting mares to run off and join their bands, enlarging the herds even further.

For the cowboy who worked on a ranch, wild horses provided sport. During slack times in the cowboy's work-a-day world, nothing was more exciting than chasing mustangs on a fast horse. When the cowboy happened to latch on to a quality wild horse, he kept it as a mount. Most wild horses, however, were sold for a mere pittance to someone who would try to tame and break them.

While most of these mustangs didn't become saddle horses because many of them were small, horses from the same base stock in Mexico were being bred for just that purpose. The Texans who took up ranching discovered that the ranchers in Mexico had established selective breeding programs with their horses — all of which traced their lineage back to the Spanish imports — and had developed high-quality horses with more size than the wild ones possessed. American ranchers turned to their Mexican counterparts to purchase saddle horses for open-range work.

The American ranchers also began crossing a few of the captured mustang mares with larger stallions from the East, including Thoroughbreds and quarter-mile sprinters from Kentucky and Tennessee.

Good horses were valuable commodities on the ranches of the 1800s because a lot of horses were needed to work cattle on hundreds of thousands of acres the ranches comprised. In the early 1900s, King Ranch in Texas, which was founded by Richard King in the mid-1800s, reportedly had a band of two thousand broodmares.

While those ranchers had little use for the wild horse as a working animal, they did find at least a niche market back East for some of the offspring of wild mares bred to larger, domestic stallions.

Carriage horses were becoming increasingly necessary as more roads were built back East. The mustang was considered too small to pull carriages or wagons but when crossed with domestic horses, the mustangs' offspring were large enough for the task.

Capturing wild horses and shipping them east didn't impact the number that continued to roam the Plains. More and more wild stallions, it seemed, were stealing domestic mares and incorporating them into their bands. In addition, of course, some domestic stallions escaped and formed their own bands of mustang mares.

While this was occurring, ranchers also had to cope with thousands of wild horses running free on the range and competing with cattle for the available grass and water. There was only one solution as far as the cattleman was concerned: kill the wild horses and the buffalo.

Though some wild horses were captured and used as stock horses, most were considered too small. In the rancher's mind, they were nuisances to be disposed of.

The war was on

Ranchers began killing off wild horses in the mid-1800s. The extermination started slowly but gained momentum as the number of cattle ranches increased. Some herds of wild horses were run into corrals and systematically gunned down. Other herds were captured and sold for a pittance to the highest bidder.

As the demand for beef increased in the eastern market, so did the need for larger cattle herds. This intensified the battle against the wild horse. Wild horses were shot, roped, pushed over cliffs and, in later years, shot from airplanes. When the pet-food market began to flourish in the early 1940s and 1950s, many of the wild horses were captured and sold to plants that turned them into dog food or fertilizer.

Still, the wild herds continued to propagate and the war continued to rage. Some descriptions of the destruction are grim. In the book, *The Wild Horse of the West*, first published in 1945, Walker D. Wyman presents this story from a cattleman.

"At that time I bought a bunch of range cattle and began to talk to other cattlemen about getting them (the wild horses) all killed off. So we started at shooting them down wherever we could…One winter…10 of us went out and run 250 over the ledge, killing all as they fell 300 feet, got them to milling on the edge of bluff till they got on sleek rocks covered with snow and all slid off. We told all the Indians they could have all they could capture so they helped to get rid of many hundreds. Early in the spring when they

Overpopulation resulted in open season on wild horses as they competed with cattle for grazing land.

(the wild horses) were poor, we could take them off a good, grain-fed horse and we would kill and catch another. None were ever shipped out, but all killed by cattlemen and now there is not one left to tell the tale (in his area). It took us about 10 years to do the job."

And through it all, cattle numbers continued to increase. In 1850 there were approximately one million cattle in seventeen western states. Only four years later that number had grown to between thirty-five million and forty million. The rangeland was over-populated and ranchers continued to get rid of wild horses that were competing with cattle for food and water.

The rancher gained another weapon in his battle against wild horses in 1874 — barbed wire. Soon vast tracts of land were fenced off, limiting the wild horses' access to both forage and water.

As the pressure to exterminate the wild horse accelerated, the wild bands retreated into less accessible areas. Nevada, with both its arid regions and the Sierra Nevada Mountains, became a stronghold for the wild bands. As late as 1910, an estimated one hundred thousand wild horses populated Nevada.

We pause to ponder the question of just what type of wild horse was roaming the Plains in the late 1800s and early 1900s. Had the addition of domestic mares and stallions into the wild bands changed the animal's look? Wyman, in his book, quotes Rufus Steele, whom he describes as a "literary mustanger." Steele provides this description:

"…they have the fine head, the slim legs, and the flowing mane and tail characteristic of the Arabian stock. They are bays, albinos, chestnuts, red and blue roans, pintos, sorrels, buckskins and milk-whites. The mares average eight hundred pounds in weight, and the stallions frequently weigh three hundred pounds more than that; they stand from thirteen to fourteen hands high. Their endurance is phenomenal, and for agility, the marks of their unshod hoofs are found at the summits of monumented boulder piles which even a mountain goat might reason-

ably be expected to cut out of his itinerary. They keep to an elevation of from six to nine thousand feet, descending to the plains hardly at all. The water holes are from twenty to fifty miles apart…Bunch-grass is their sustenance in summer; then the first frosts cure the white sage, and as that becomes palatable, they paw through the snow to reach it, and keep fat throughout the winter."

If the mustanger's assessment of weight was correct, the domestic horses may have been responsible for increasing the size of at least some of the wild horses.

While the rugged high country was a stronghold for the wild horses of Nevada, it still was not safe from man. In 1900 Nevada's state legislature enacted a law that allowed the killing of all wild and unbranded horses on the range. Wyman reports in his book that "within a year or two, about 15,000 horses had been shot, and the hides and bounties had more than paid for the efforts."

When ranchers first started killing wild horses, the public voiced little opposition. Many people in the fast-growing West considered wild horses as nothing more than vermin. In the East, people seemed unaware of the campaign against the wild horses. That was about to change.

On February 19, 1908, from Reno, Nevada, the Associated Press filed two apparently inaccurate stories that many newspapers printed. The stories, which reported that state and federal rangers were to begin killing off wild horses, roused public sentiment against the killings that would grow steadily as the years went by and the slaughter continued.

The first story read as follows:

"A campaign to exterminate the wild horses in the Toyabe, Toquima, and Monito forest reserves in Lander County has been started, and it is believed that more than fifteen thousand wild horses now grazing on these preserves will be slaughtered before another year passes.

"The forest rangers report that there are more

than 15,000 wild horses on these ranges and that they are attracting many domestic animals to the district. The horses destroy the vegetation and do much harm to the entire district, consequently a war of extermination will be waged against them."

The second story was more succinct, but probably stirred greater interest because now the U.S. government was also allegedly ordering the slaughter of horses:

"The forestry department at Washington has ordered the rangers to kill all wild horses on the government domain."

Americans did then as Americans do now when they do not agree with a governmental decision. They wrote letters by the thousands, protesting the U.S. Forest Service's reported edict.

The Forest Service claimed that it was all a mistake. Each of the letter writers received this reply, in part: "No orders have been issued by the Forest Service for killing horses upon any of the National Forests. The report originated in an unwarranted press dispatch given out through the newspapers of the country."

Though the Forest Service's reply might have cooled some heated passions, the plight of the wild horse had piqued the public's interest, and many stood ready to argue that the wild horses had as much right to rangeland as did a rancher's cattle.

Actually, the federal government would not be involved with programs to control animal populations on public lands until 1934 when Congress passed what became known as the Taylor Grazing Act, which put the Department of Interior in charge of administering how open rangeland was used.

That action was stimulated by a rising tide of public and political opinion that the range was being overused and abused, which it was, and that controls were needed. No longer would cattlemen be allowed to run unlimited numbers of livestock, and no longer would the range be available to the ranchers free of charge.

This only stimulated ranchers' desire to get rid of the wild horse. The more wild horses on a piece of public property meant fewer cattle allowed by the Bureau of Land Management, which had been created to enforce rangeland rules and regulations.

So, the war against the wild horse continued, but so did support for their plight. Change did not come rapidly because most people in the United States were not familiar with wild horses and the methods used to capture and ship them to slaughter. During the 1950s, stories began to appear in popular magazines about the sometimes inhumane capture and transport of wild horses. As word began to spread nationwide concerning these practices, more and more people rallied to the wild horse cause. Horse protection organizations were created, many of which are still active today.

A most effective and zealous supporter of the wild horses was Velma Johnston, of Reno, Nevada, who became the first president of the International Society for the Protection of Mustangs and Burros. Velma was born and raised in Nevada. She was one of four children in a family that believed in kind and humane treatment for all animals. Velma suffered polio as a youth and it left her with a twisted body. Often ridiculed by others her age, she devoted a good deal of time to animals. As an adult, she launched her campaign for wild horse protection in 1951 after observing a truckload of horses in transit to slaughter. She was appalled by their poor condition and by the way they were being handled. She watched in horror as a foal in the truck was trampled to death by two stallions.

Velma lobbied Congress with vigor and with emotion, seeking an end to the continuing slaughter of wild horses. Velma was especially opposed to using airplanes to drive horses into traps. She became known as "Wild Horse Annie." Her first success came in 1959 when Congress passed what became known as the Wild Horse Annie Act. It specifically forbade using airplanes to haze wild horses.

While the Wild Horse Annie Act was a legislative

milestone, it did not result in wide-scale changes in the capturing and shipping of wild horses. There was nothing in the 1959 legislation that stated that the wild horses were public property under protection of the federal government. It merely stated that using aircraft or motorized vehicles to capture wild horses was an offense punishable under federal law. As a result, wild horse roundups in one form or another continued almost unabated.

By now, however, more people had become interested in the wild horses' plight, and horse protection groups initiated letter-writing campaigns to public officials. These groups also sent members to Washington to lobby for their cause. It took some time, but ultimately they were successful.

The second and most important piece of legislation protecting wild horses was enacted in 1971. It is officially known as Public Law 92-195 and is titled the Wild and Free Roaming Horse and Burro Act. That piece of legislation forbids private citizens from harassing, capturing, or killing wild horses.

"Congress," states the preamble to the act, "finds and declares that wild free-roaming horses and burros are living symbols of the historic and pioneer spirit of the west."

The wild horses were finally protected, but not before the population was severely depleted. Instead of hundreds of thousands of wild horses roaming the West today, the number has dropped to about forty thousand, which reside in ten western states. And even that number, says the Bureau of Land Management, is too many. Officials say that the habitat of the wild horse herds in the West can properly support only about half that number.

Several approaches have been employed to cut down the numbers, such as rounding up wild horses and offering them for adoption to private citizens for a token amount. Some birth-control procedures have also been considered.

And, as usual, there is controversy. Animal rights groups argue that the wild horse has more right to the rangeland than do ranchers' cattle. Cattlemen state that wild horses are consuming a limited supply of forage and water that could be put to better use with his livestock. Though the cattleman still wants the wild horses removed from rangeland, he no longer can legally take action on his own to get the job done.

To this point, we have been concerned with tracing the history of what has become known as the western horse as it developed in the Southwest and West, both as a domestic animal and one living in the wild. However, on the other side of the continent, along the eastern seaboard, colonists were also involved with breeding horses that would impact the western horse.

The Western Horse in the East

4

To comprehend how the western horse developed in America, we must first understand how horses developed in England. Historians tell us that in 55 B.C. the invading Romans were opposed by English warriors in chariots equipped with scythes fastened to the axle ends. The fearsome fighting machines were driven into their adversaries' midst at high speed, pulled by small, compact, and speedy horses.

The Romans, however, ultimately overpowered their opponents and occupied England for the next five hundred years. They also ruled much of the world at this time, making it reasonable to assume that they transported horses to England from such places as Gaul (modern-day France and Belgium), Italy, and Spain. The likely result is that horses larger than the native ponies that had pulled the war chariots arrived in England during Roman rule.

Historians say the Romans probably raced in Britain on a considerable scale. They also bred horses for two-horse chariot racing, which went on throughout the Roman Empire. Thus, it can be assumed that horses shipped to Britain from mainland Europe were light and speedy.

Based on the sturdy roads that were constructed, the Romans probably also imported heavier draft horses from Europe.

Roman rule ended in England about 410 A.D. Many years of war and strife followed as landowners fought for control of territory while fighting off new waves of invaders. Little is known about the development of the horse in England during those turbulent years other than that it was used in war. It wasn't until peace and prosperity descended in the early 1500s, and leisure time increased, that the horse became prominent on the English sporting scene.

During the reign of Henry VIII (1509–1547), a light-horse breed was developed in England. The king ordered that "weedy" stallions be destroyed to prevent them from reproducing. He decreed that persons of a particular station in life should keep a certain type of stallion. He also established the Royal Studs, farms around England at which quality horses were bred and raised.

At about the same time, the Spanish government presented the English with some Barbs, a light, courageous breed from north Africa that the Moors introduced into Spain. Other Barbs arrived by way of Italy. Some of these imports were crossed with the English horses in an effort to breed lighter horses that could run swiftly and participate in a variety of equine sports.

The imports were more beautiful animals than some of the western European horses, which were bigger, with larger heads and a more sluggish nature.

The monarchs after Henry VIII — Elizabeth, James I, and Charles I — had great interest in horses. During their reigns, the prominent citizens of England "discovered" the sport horse and racing began to flourish. Racecourses were developed near a number of towns and cities. Among the more famous were those at Chester, Salisbury, Croydon, Richmond, Doncaster, and Newmarket. Monarchs themselves or city officials often presented the trophy, usually a bell, for feature races.

King James I, who occupied the throne in the early 1600s, took his penchant for the sporting life to an extreme. He built a home at Newmarket and spent much of his time there. In 1621 the House of Commons petitioned him not to put his pleasures at Newmarket before his public duties. It apparently had little effect on the monarch, who loved to hunt and gamble on horse races. He continued his dogged pursuit of the sporting life until 1625, when he became ill after a hunting trip to Newmarket and died.

His successor, Charles I, also neglected state affairs for love of hunting and racing. Parliament, with its ruling Puritan element, decided to put a damper on the king's activities by shutting down race meetings and even ordering Newmarket Heath ploughed up to prevent hunting.

In 1649 Parliament ordered Charles I beheaded for treason, and Oliver Cromwell came to power first as commander in chief of the army and then served as Lord Protector, or head of Parliament, from 1653 until his death in 1658. During his rule, Cromwell closed down the Royal Studs. Some of the horses at the studs went to Ireland, and Cromwell kept some for himself, breeding for cavalry chargers rather than racing.

The monarchy was restored in 1660, and the British returned to racing with an enthusiasm that quickly made up for lost time. The new monarch, Charles II, not only bred and trained racehorses but he also developed a legendary reputation as a jockey. In 1675 he won the Newmarket Plate, thus becoming the only British monarch ever to win a race.

The race meets of those days were times of *joie de vivre*. The diarist John Evelyn, who visited Newmarket in October 1671, found "the jolly blades, racing, dancing, feasting and reveling more resem-

bling a luxurious and abandoned rout, than a Christian court."

The landed gentry also discovered fox hunting. This sport, which involved following hounds in pursuit of a fox, demanded athletic horses that could race through field and forest and sail over fences.

During the reign of Charles II (1660–1685), horse racing became entrenched in English culture. Charles II was interested in all sports, but he was most passionate about those that involved the horse. He directed that Arabians be procured for the Royal Stud. This indirectly led to the later importation of three stallions that would become the foundation sires of the Thoroughbred breed. They were known as the Byerley Turk, the Darley Arabian, and the Godolphin Arabian.

There is little comprehensive information about the Byerley Turk. According to one account, when Budapest was captured from the Turks in 1686, the stallion was taken as a spoil of war by a Captain Byerley and sent to England. The Byerley Turk was described as being dark bay, easy to handle, and extremely fast.

The Darley Arabian, foaled in 1700, was described as being a horse of exceptional beauty. He came from Aleppo in Syria, where it was believed the finest Arabians were bred. Thomas Darley, who was serving England as consul to Aleppo, procured the Darley Arabian. The story goes that Darley traded a rifle for the three-year-old colt and sent him to his father, Sir Richard Darley, in Yorkshire. The horse grew to fifteen hands, which was considered tall for an Arabian.

The Godolphin Arabian was foaled in 1724. He is the subject of much folklore. The story goes that he was discovered in a thin and woebegone condition drawing a water cart on the streets of Paris after having been sold by King Louis XVI. The French king had received the Godolphin Arabian and three other horses as gifts from the Bey of Tunis. The king had no appreciation for the eastern horses and ordered all four to be sold. The Godolphin Arabian was reportedly rescued from the water cart by an Englishman identified as Mr. Coke. The horse, described as having a difficult temperament, eventually wound up in the hands of Lord Godolphin. At his stable, the rescued stallion served as a teaser for an important sire named Hobgoblin. Legend says that the Godolphin Arabian fought Hobgoblin for the mare Roxana and won. He then covered her, and the result was the famed stallion Cade.

The three imported stallions continued to be bred to descendants of Barb mares imported earlier by Charles II and some domestic English mares. Each foundation stallion is responsible for a sire line that still plays an important role in Thoroughbred breeding. The sire lines were developed through Matchem, descending from the Godolphin Arabian; Eclipse, from the Darley Arabian; and Herod, from the Byerley Turk.

Matchem a son of Cade, stood only 14.3 hands but was fast and had great endurance. Races often were run in heats, and there were times when Matchem would compete in three heats of four miles, all in one day. He lived to age thirty-three and during his lifetime sired 354 winners. The great Man o' War would be one of many outstanding racehorses that traced their lineage back to Matchem.

Eclipse was so named because he was foaled on April 5, 1764, a day when England witnessed a full solar eclipse. The name would become totally appropriate because not only did the stallion "eclipse" his competitors on the racetrack, where he was undefeated, he also "eclipsed" them in the breeding shed. An estimated ninety percent of today's Thoroughbreds descend in their direct male line from this outstanding stallion.

Herod, a descendant of the Byerley Turk, was described as being well built and muscled. He raced from age five to nine and was defeated only twice. At stud, he sired 497 winners.

Thus, we can see that the ultimate development

Eclipse had a profound influence on the American Thoroughbred, and hence the western horse.

of the Thoroughbred as a breed was based heavily on Arabian, Barb, and Turk blood, though some Galloway, Hobby, and Highland Dun blood was involved as well.

The three original foundation stallions differed in type. It is important to look at each, because the melding of their bloodlines, plus crossing their descendants with other breeds, has significantly influenced the development of the western horse.

Colonel John F. Wall, a retired U.S. cavalryman who wrote the 1950 book *Breeding Thoroughbreds*, proffered descriptions of the Arabian, the Barb, and the Turk. He starts with the Arabian:

"The best Arabs average 14½ hands and weigh from 800 to 1,000 pounds. The head is intelligent, well-formed, and set on the neck at such an angle as to allow high head carriage; the face is concave (dish-faced) from opposite the eye to the nostrils, being wide across the forehead and narrow at the muzzle, the eyes are large, kind, expressive and prominent…The bone of the Arabian horse is dense and ligaments and tendons are usually well placed and defined. The Arab is well coupled, having a short back and well-sprung ribs, but the body is more or less round; the croup is level but smooth; the quarters are wide and strong and the gaskins are large, while the hocks are well let down. The tail is usually set on high and carried high."

Next, we turn to his description of the Barb. As mentioned earlier, the Spanish conquistadors used horses that likely had a good deal of Barb blood:

"The Barb is defined to be a 'horse of the breed introduced by the Moors from Barbary into Spain, and are noted for speed and endurance.'

"The maximum height of the Barb does not ordinarily exceed 14½ hands. He is, in general, coarser than the Arab. The face is more or less convex compared to the face of the Arab; ears are often 'flop,' the neck is more arched, the shoulder is flatter and perhaps more oblique, the withers are more prominent, the pasterns are longer and the chest is deeper than

in the Arab. The Barb has powerful loins; the arms and quarters are muscular. He is often goose-rumped. His feet are well open at the heels."

It is generally believed that the Godolphin Arabian was a Barb.

Now for Wall's description of the Turk:

"The Turk is said to be derived from a mixture of Arab, Persian and perhaps other native breeds of Western Asia. These horses are taller and more leggy than the Arab, frequently being 15 to 16 hands. The Turk is similar to our race horse in general build. He is hardy, courageous and active.

"The designation of 'Turk,' often applied to early eastern horses is perhaps due to circumstances of acquisition. Many of the importations were probably of Arabian origin, but were obtained in one way or another by the English from the Turks."

Considering that the first horses sent to America from England arrived in 1609, it is highly unlikely that those imports looked like the Thoroughbred we know today or like the three types described by Wall because they had not yet appeared on the scene.

One can assume that the first imports contained native Hobby blood and some Galloway blood. The latter breed developed in Galloway, Scotland. The Hobby developed in Ireland.

The progenitors of the Galloway are said to have escaped from Spanish ships driven ashore by the English. The Galloways were crossed with native horses, and the progeny were called Scotch Galloways, a now-extinct breed.

The Galloway horses were reportedly about fourteen hands, bright bay or brown with black legs, small heads, and clean limbs. They were described as gentle but fast and extremely tough. It is more likely that the colonists would bring horses of this type to the New World rather than the more exotic equines that the ruling class was developing.

In a historical context, the type of horses first imported to Jamestown in 1609 matters little because none survived. Starving colonists ate some, while

Native Americans killed the rest.

Some years would pass before imported horses would become important to the early colonists. As in medieval times, oxen were believed more practical and economical for farming. Colonists used horses primarily to pack goods between inland settlements and riverboats.

In many of the colonies horses were not bred in appreciable numbers until the late 1600s, some sixty to seventy years after the first colonists arrived.

For New England colonists horse ownership had some negative associations. The Puritans considered horses expensive to keep and took a dim view of horseback riding, an activity favored by the landed gentry of England. That was enough to turn off the Puritans, who had left those oppressive landowners behind in pursuit of a new life in America. Though it took time, that prejudice finally waned and disappeared. Eventually, Americans looked to England as a source for quality horses, especially stallions.

Some of the earliest imports from England to the United States can be traced to Charles I. Many of his loyal followers, fearing for their own heads, escaped to the New World. They brought with them some of their good horses and later had others shipped over. Many of the newcomers settled in Virginia and quickly turned it into a horse-breeding center.

The Thoroughbred had not been established as a breed at the time, though there were efforts to create an English racehorse. One of the early racing-type horses imported from England was Tamerlane, a stallion William Penn brought to the Colonies in 1699. However, the horse's bloodline faded and eventually was lost.

The first Thoroughbred-type stallion imported to America was Bulle Rock, who arrived from England in 1730 at age twenty-one. Sired by the Darley Arabian and out of a daughter of the Byerley Turk, Bulle Rock served as a progenitor of both Thoroughbreds and Quarter Horses in the United States.

Many similar horses followed in Bulle Rock's wake. Many Virginians became wealthy by raising tobacco and marketing it in England. With the proceeds, many of the plantation owners had agents in England procure and send over a stallion and mare or two. Something of a "keep up with the Joneses" mentality existed. If a plantation owner imported an exceptionally good horse, his peers would do the same so that they wouldn't be losers at the track. Some great horses were imported between 1730 and 1751. In addition to Bulle Rock they include Dabster in 1742, Monkey in 1737, Jolly Roger in 1751, Traveler in 1748, Silver Eye and Childers in 1756, and, perhaps the greatest of them all, Janus in 1751.

Janus, a foundation sire of the Quarter Horse.

The last-named would have a significant impact on the development of the western horse as a founding sire of the Quarter Horse.

The colonists in the Carolinas also began importing horses and launching their own breeding programs and race meets. However, the Revolutionary War brought an end to commerce with England. War shut off importation of horses though demand only increased as the colonists sought to combat the English cavalry, whose horses were shipped from England, procured from Loyalists in America, or confiscated in raids.

The British approach during the Revolutionary War was to secure a good harbor and use it for a base. They would send out soldiers from there to procure supplies and animals. If the port were in a part of the country inhabited by Loyalists, the British would merely purchase the horses and supplies from the inhabitants. Often the Loyalists would bring their animals and produce to selected villages, and the purchasing, trading, and bartering with the British soldiers would be carried out in a central location. If the base were in an area filled with patriots, the British often sent out mounted raiders to take what they wanted. If the base were in a neutral area, the British would go from farm to farm, seeking to purchase horses and supplies.

The British, in addition to confiscating horses, also killed others to keep them out of patriot hands. For example, the British captured three sons of a celebrated running horse named Old Bacchus and drowned them in the York River in Virginia. The British also were held responsible for the death of a celebrated mare named Nancy Wake.

British cavalry officer Bonastre "Bloody" Tarleton was a scourge in the southern Colonies, capturing all good horses he could find and turning them into mounts for his cavalry, in addition to plundering and pillaging. Other horses, of course, were lost in battle. By war's end, the horse populations in Virginia, New York, Pennsylvania, and the Carolinas had been decimated. It would take some time in the wake of the war to re-establish breeding centers and increase the equine population.

During the Revolution, however, the colonists had continued to breed horses. Many had already launched programs that did not immediately involve English imports. Their prime equine sources were two Native American tribes — the Chickasaw and the Cherokee — both of which had been breeding horses with bloodlines based on Spanish imports to Mexico.

The colonists called these horses Chickasaws. That name would stick even though some of the horses were from the Cherokees. The Chickasaws had gotten their horses from the Spanish settlements that extended south from Georgia into Florida, and the Cherokees had procured theirs from Spanish settlements in the Southwest, as well as the Southeast.

The small and solid Chickasaw horses were surefooted and had endurance. They could run short distances very fast and became America's first racehorses. They were versatile as well, with the ability to pull a plow, serve as a riding horse, and be hitched to a carriage. Later the Chickasaws were crossed with the English imports to produce a horse taller and prettier than the Chickasaw but with the same type of stamina and strength.

While farms in Virginia and the Carolinas were breeding horses for racing, draft breeds were being developed in New York and Pennsylvania. The Dutch who settled these areas had preferred horses to oxen from the very beginning and had brought some horses with them from the old country. After William Penn founded Pennsylvania in 1682, he brought over thousands of farmers from the lower Rhine River Valley. These Germans, or Pennsylvania Dutch, also favored the horse over the oxen and concentrated on improving the breeding of their draft animals.

Horse racing became popular in colonial America in the late 1600s and early 1700s for the same reason it had become popular in England some years before. There was more wealth and leisure time. In the early days, races were confined to rough dirt strips only fifteen or twenty feet wide, from which the brush and large rocks had been removed. The contests were match races involving two horses running on parallel paths. During the race, each horse was to run on its designated path without ever crossing to the other horse's path. There was an open space at both start and finish lines to allow for a walkup start and space to pull up the running horses after they flashed past the judges, or "end men."

Village greens and streets also became popular racing venues. However, village leaders would soon decide that racing down the streets was too dangerous for the citizenry. In Jamestown, Virginia, for example, the city fathers in 1676 banned racing on the streets.

No matter the location, these races were often rough and tumble affairs with jockeys grabbing on to each other and battling all the way down the track. There also are reports of finish-line judges being bribed. Nevertheless, a racing meet was a festive occasion that included drinking, feasting, dancing, and gambling.

The sprinting racehorses came to be called Quarter-Pathers because most of the races were run on quarter mile tracks or "paths." They later came to be called Celebrated American Quarter Running Horses.

As crowds grew, entertaining innovations were added to the races. In one type of race, for example, the last horse to cross the finish line was declared the winner. However, there was a catch. Each contestant had to ride an opponent's horse. Thus, the only way a competitor could ensure that his horse would not be first across the line was to outrun it on the horse he was riding.

By the time the Revolutionary War ended, sprint racing had pretty much evaporated in the southern colonies because longer races were now in vogue in that part of the country. When racing was revived after the war, it took place on long, oval tracks that favored the more leggy horses being bred in Virginia and the Carolinas. The longer races were patterned after those being run in England.

However, sprint racing hadn't really disappeared; it was simply changing location. Settlers were heading west in great numbers, and they were taking muscled horses suited for sprinting with them.

As the seaboard settlements began bursting at the seams, the settlers pushed farther inland. Before long they had moved to the base of the Blue Ridge Mountains in Virginia in the first westward migration. The "West" of those days was across the Appalachian Mountains in areas that would become Tennessee, Kentucky, and Ohio. The settlers moved up the Mohawk Valley into northern Ohio. They traveled what was known as the Forbes Road and the Cumberland Road until they came to the Ohio River. Then, they followed the river down to country that, up until then, had been occupied only by Native American tribes.

During the late 1770s and early 1780s, more than 100,000 pioneer families from New England and the South headed into the virgin lands of the "West." The pioneers traveled any way they could — carrying their belongings on their backs, using oxen and horses to pull wagons, and riding both horses and mules. Once the pioneers reached their destinations, the horses, mules, and oxen were put to work uprooting stumps and pulling plows.

The settlers had brought with them solidly muscled horses that could perform a variety of tasks. They used these horses first to clear land and then to plant crops. After the settlers established homesteads and villages, they once again sought pleasures like horse racing. It wasn't long before sprint tracks were being hacked out of the forests. The first track in Kentucky, located in what is now Lexington, was established in 1780.

And, interestingly, what did the newcomers also find in this new, unsettled land?

Wild horses.

Bands of wild horses ranged through the foothills of the new frontier, trampling through grain fields and damaging orchards. These bands likely originated from horses that escaped from the Native American tribes populating the area.

The law permitted any farmer to shoot without penalty any wild horse that entered his orchard for the third time. As would happen in the far West some years later, horses became hunted animals in the wake of the white man's arrival. And just as would also happen later in the far West, some of the wild horses were captured and trained to be ridden or driven, but most were considered to be of inferior quality and were simply destroyed.

Colonial Travel

In the Colonies' early days, most settlers had traveled by water. Sometimes they would put out to sea, round a point, and arrive at a neighboring oceanfront settlement. They also traveled by boat along streams and tidewater estuaries.

It wasn't long, however, before roads were being hacked through forests and over hill and dale. The roads allowed travel by horseback and later, as the quality of the roads continued to improve, by private and public coaches.

In 1783 the last British troops left the Colonies and sailed home. Once more, people were able to move freely from New England to New York and on through to places like Philadelphia and Baltimore. With heightened travel came the need to get there faster.

The same year that the British troops left the colonies, a man named Levi Pease established a stage service between Boston, Massachusetts, and Hartford, Connecticut, a distance of a little more than 120 miles. He started with two wagons, each pulled by four horses. The trip took about four days with stopovers in towns along the way. In 1784, the route was extended to New York.

In 1785, Congress established a postal service, and Pease was awarded the first contract to carry mail between Boston and New York. He used light wagons instead of post riders and promised delivery in five and a half days in winter and four days in summer. As roads improved, that time was cut to one and a half days. But even with improved roads, teams had to be changed every ten miles to cover the distance that quickly. In addition to mail, each wagon could carry four passengers. The mail contract proved so profitable that Pease soon extended his service for both mail and passengers to other New England towns. As others entered the transportation business, a variety of coaches soon were traveling the country.

Now even more horses, particularly heavier horses, were needed to carry riders and to pull the growing number of carriages and stagecoaches. While draft horses remained in demand, some of the stallions were bred to Chickasaw and Chickasaw-cross mares to produce a powerful horse but one lighter and quicker of foot. Rather than the huge draft horses that could tip the scales between 1,800 and 2,000 pounds, these new hybrids weighed between 1,100 and 1,200 pounds. The lighter animals were desired as coach horses.

If a light carriage was used for travel, a team of two horses often was sufficient to pull it. If the conveyance was larger and heavier but the travel over level terrain, a four-horse hitch would be employed. If the larger vehicle was to travel through rugged hill country, a six-horse hitch might be in order.

Coach travel greatly improved when the first of the famous Concord coaches, which were light and durable and completely enclosed, arrived in 1826. The coaches were manufactured in Concord, New Hampshire. Prior to the Concord, most coaches during the preceding forty years were wagons with light tops and leather side curtains. The Concord would be the standard for horse-drawn coaches for seventy years.

Advances in travel helped pave the way for the great westward migration that would follow.

The Great Westward Migration

5

The beautiful and rugged western landscape attracted adventurous settlers looking for land and opportunity.

It began with the bargain-basement special of all time. In 1803 President Thomas Jefferson purchased the Louisiana Territory from France for $15 million. Neither party in the transaction was sure exactly how much land was involved, but they did know that the area stretched from the Mississippi River north to the Canadian border and west into the Rocky Mountains. The purchase doubled the size of the United States.

It was a huge area that included towering mountains, vast plains covered by seas of tall grass, forests filled with towering trees, and rushing rivers, all of it teeming with wildlife.

At the time, few people knew anything about the area. Ships had visited the West Coast, but thousands of miles and millions of acres between the Atlantic and the Pacific remained unexplored. Only Native Americans and the occasional trapper inhabited this vast expanse.

The brilliant and visionary Jefferson wanted desperately to learn about the mysterious West. Was there a waterway that could be used as a link? He had to know.

He commissioned Meriwether Lewis and William Clark to lead a band of explorers across the new land. They traveled up the Missouri River until mountains blocked their waterway.

The expedition did not have enough horses for a trek over the imposing mountains. The few horses it did have came from the Mandan Indians, with whom the expedition had spent its first winter.

In need of more horses to carry scientific equipment, supplies, and trading goods, the expedition was lucky enough to hire a French-Canadian interpreter whose sixteen-year-old pregnant wife, Sacajawea, was Shoshone. Known for her calmness and self-possession, Sacajawea accompanied her husband on the expedition. She guided the explorers to her tribe, of which her brother was one of the leaders.

The explorers obtained twenty-nine horses from the Shoshones, who had recently lost part of their herd in a raid by another tribe and were probably unwilling to part with any quality animals.

The available horses sufficed as pack animals, and with a few more acquired from the Flathead Indians in Bitterroot Valley, the expedition managed to struggle across the mountains, fighting bad weather and sometimes treacherous trails along the way.

Once across the mountains, the trekkers encountered the Nez Perce Indians and discovered this tribe owned selectively bred horses. Many of these handsome horses would become the foundation of what one day would be called the Appaloosa.

Lewis praised the Nez Perce's horses in his journal:

"Their horses appear to be of an excellent race: they are lofty, eligantly (sic) formed, active and durable: in short, many of them look like the fine English coarsers (sic) and would make a figure in any country. Some of those horses are pided (pied) with large spots of white irregularly scattered and intermixed with the black, brown or bey (bay) or some other dark colour, but much the larger portion are of an uniform color with stars, snips and white feet, or in this rispect (sic) marked much like our best blooded horses in Virginia, which they resemble as well in fleetness and bottom as in form and colours.

"The natives suffer them to run at large in the plains, the grass of which furnishes them with their only subsistence their masters taking no trouble to lay in a winters store for them, but they even keep fat if not much used on the dry grass of the plains during the winter."

Lewis also discovered many Native American tribes preferred mules. Several tribes, he wrote in

The Appaloosa, developed by the Nez Perce Indians, caught the attention of Lewis and Clark.

his journal, "have also a great number of mules, which among the Indians I find are much more highly prized than horses.

"An eligant (sic) horse," he continued, "may be purchased of the natives in this country for a few peads (few beads) or other paltry trinkets which in the U' States would not cost more than one or two dollars.

"This abundance and cheapness of horses will be extremely advantageous to those who may hereafter attempt the fir (fur) trade to the East Indies by way of the Columbia River and the Pacific Ocean."

The mules and some of the horses owned by these natives, Lewis opined, had been stolen "from the Spaniards of Mexico." He wrote in his journal that several horses belonging to a tribe on the upper southeast fork of the Columbia River were carrying Spanish brands "which we supposed had been stolen from the inhabitants of Mexico."

Lewis and Clark left their own thirty-eight horses with the Nez Perce while they journeyed toward the Pacific in canoes. They picked up their horses the following spring and once again crossed the Bitterroot Mountains, this time heading back toward civilization. But as the expedition moved down the Missouri by boat various tribes stole all of the horses as they were being herded along the river.

The Lewis and Clark expedition opened the gates for immigrants to move to the far West. In the beginning it was just mountain men, who were looking for solitude and furs. They would be the trailblazers, but soon hundreds of thousands of people would head west, seeking a new life and cheap land. Beginning in the 1840s and continuing

Wagon trains by the hundreds lined up for the western land rushes.

for the next several decades, hundreds of wagon trains traveled west, providing the opportunity for eastern horses to mingle with those from the West and Southwest.

People following their dreams to the far West traveled in a variety of ways, but most loaded their belongings in covered wagons pulled by oxen, horses, or mules. Some groups making the trek west were large. The largest on record traveled from Kansas in 1843 and was dubbed "The Great Migration." There were more than 100 wagons and about 250 men, 130 women, and 610 children. There also were some 5,000 head of cattle, which were herded along by mounted horsemen.

As more and more of the frontier became settled, the trafficking of horses from east to west and west to east increased. Many horse traders traveled along the Santa Fe Trail, which ran from New Mexico to Missouri over a thousand miles of rugged terrain. Despite the potential for disaster, which also included being raided by Native Americans, some entrepreneurs decided the dangers were worth the risk. Their goal was to obtain horses in California from Mexican rancheros and trail them to eastern markets where, hopefully, they would sell at a profit. California had become a horse-raising hotbed in the early to mid-1800s as the rancheros produced far more horses than could be used locally. This changed after the United States went to war with Mexico and emerged the victor. With the Treaty of Guadalupe Hidalgo, California and New Mexico became part of the United States in February 1848, the year gold was discovered in California.

In 1849 thousands of Americans made their way to the gold fields and many stayed. The horse surplus in California quickly disappeared.

One adventurer, Ewing Young, first traveled to California in 1830 to procure mules for the eastern markets. However, he discovered that mules were in short supply and commanded high prices, so he purchased fifteen hundred horses instead and trailed them all the way to Missouri.

This group of horses added a new strain of Spanish stock to the bloodlines being raised in the Ohio River Valley and other eastern areas.

Miles Goodyear, a fur trapper turned horse trader, conducted one of the most celebrated horse drives. In April 1848, he bought 231 horses in California and set out for Fort Leavenworth, Kansas, where he planned to sell them to the U.S. army for use in the Mexican War. When he reached Fort Leavenworth some two thousand miles later, he learned, to his dismay, that the war had ended and there was no ready market for his horses. However, news of the gold strike near Sutter's Mill in California reached Goodyear about that time. He decided in a flash that the thousands of miners flocking to California would soon use up all of the available horses there. He turned around and headed back toward California with his string of horses. By the time he arrived in Sacramento, his horses had traveled a grand total of four thousand miles.

Another young man, Philip Nolan, tried to capitalize on the horse trade in the South and Southwest, though a dubious reputation as a fortune seeker preceded the native of Ireland. In 1790, while living in New Orleans, he secured some trade goods, a passport, and a commission from the Spanish province's governor to provide the local Spanish troops with horses from Texas.

Unfortunately for Nolan, the Spanish authorities in Texas not only refused to honor his passport, they confiscated all of his trade goods as well. Nolan slipped off and spent two years living with the Native Americans. In 1793 he made another foray into Texas. This time he evaded the Spanish authorities in Texas and came back with fifty horses. In 1794, with a new passport and six companions, he again went to Texas and returned with 250 horses. His next venture was in 1797, when he brought back 1,300 horses to Louisiana.

His luck ran out in 1800 when he was intercepted in Texas by Spanish authorities who correctly suspected that Nolan was up to mischief other than merely procuring horses. It was learned later that Nolan was involved with Aaron Burr and General James Wilkinson in their scheme to invade Spanish territory and found a new nation. Nolan chose to fight rather than surrender and was killed by a cannonball.

Nolan's story is significant because he was one of many such traders who sought to procure cheap horses in the West and sell them for a profit in the East.

Many of these entrepreneurs bought horses legitimately in places like Texas and California where they were plentiful. Still others gathered up wild horses to which no one had title. However, on many occasions tame horses owned by ranchers were gathered up along with some of the wild ones or just outright stolen.

The horse trade between West and East increased when a 1795 treaty between the United States and Spain opened the way for the United States to ship goods through New Orleans. Heavily laden flatboats from the Ohio River Valley would make their way down the Ohio-Mississippi River system, arriving in New Orleans.

The boat crews would then return to Natchez, Mississippi, where they would buy horses that had come from the West and Southwest. The horses would be driven back to the Ohio River Valley country along the Natchez Trace, a well-traveled trail that ran between Natchez, Mississippi, and Nashville, Tennessee. This greatly increased the flow of horses from the western plains to eastern markets. It also enabled the settlers west of the Allegheny Mountains to purchase horses at modest prices and not have to compete in the eastern marketplace, where horses were much needed for stage lines, freight lines, and riding mounts.

Entrepreneurial easterners were realizing they could make money breeding horses out West and selling them back East. Among them was A.C. Huidekoper of Meadville, Pennsylvania, whose story typifies the back and forth movement of equines throughout the 1800s.

Huidekoper and three companions traveled to North Dakota to hunt buffalo in 1879. During their stay, Huidekoper and his companions concluded that the rich prairie grass in and around the North

The western stagecoach flourished until the railroad made it obsolete.

Dakota Badlands would make excellent grazing range for cattle. The next year they formed the Custer Trail Cattle Company.

Huidekoper did not want to raise just run-of-the-mill cattle. He wanted quality. He bought some of the best cows he could find in Minnesota and also purchased a railcar-load of "full-blooded shorthorn bulls" in the East.

He decided almost simultaneously to become a player in the horse trading game, again using high-quality stock. His goal was to become one of the country's major suppliers of both saddle horses and draft horses. He imported thirty-five purebred Percheron mares and six stallions from France to found his draft horse program.

To improve some of the native ranch horse stock, which tended to be on the small side, he turned to the Thoroughbred.

He purchased a gray grandson of the celebrated Lexington as his key stallion. The horse's registered name was Bound, but because of his color, the North Dakota cowboys called him Grey Wolf. Huidekoper bought Grey Wolf as a four-year-old. The horse had been only moderately successful on the racetrack but Huidekoper knew that Grey Wolf at 15.3 hands would add some speed and size to his stock. Huidekoper described Grey Wolf as a "wonderful sire" and turned him loose among a large harem of mares and used the resulting offspring as mounts for his cowboys.

Shortly after purchasing Grey Wolf, Huidekoper bought a group of mares that the army had captured from Sitting Bull.

"I bought some of these," Huidekoper wrote in a journal, "to cross on my Thoroughbred stallion. Some of these ponies had bullet holes through their necks received in the Custer fight." (The massacre of General George A. Custer's Seventh Cavalry at the Little Big Horn in June 1876.)

Crossing Grey Wolf with the Native American ponies was profitable for Huidekoper. A number of the offspring were sold in the East as polo ponies. Huidekoper proudly wrote that one of them sold for $1,500 and another for $2,500. He referred to the Thoroughbred–Native American pony cross as the American Horse. Many of the Indian ponies were bald-faced and passed this characteristic marking to their offspring. Others were spotted, and still others were solid-colored. Because Grey Wolf carried gray genes, many of his offspring were gray.

Huidekoper's herd grew until it reached about four thousand. Because of his connections in the East, he continued to market horses there.

Eastern and western bloodlines were continually commingled to meet the equine needs of a country expanding west. Breeding programs were started to produce horses to fulfill certain needs, such as pull stagecoaches, herd cattle, or carry mail for the Pony Express.

In 1858 the post office awarded a mail contract to the Butterfield Overland Mail Company. The company sold the government on its plan to run a stage line 2,800 miles from St. Louis to San Francisco in twenty-five days.

For openers, the company bought one hundred Concord coaches, one thousand horses, and about five hundred mules. They selected a southern route for the stagecoaches to avoid high mountains and heavy snows. The route crossed the Southwest through El Paso and Tucson and on to the San Joaquin Valley and from there into San Francisco.

To make the trip in the twenty-five days stipulated in the contract, a series of stage stations stocked with fresh horses had to be established along the way. The teams left behind would be rested and then put back into the rotation.

The smaller horses of the western Plains were not powerful enough to pull the stagecoaches. Larger horses were needed from the East. In some cases, they were the product of draft horses crossed with lighter animals. This "in-between" horse was strong enough to pull the coach but could travel faster and longer than the large draft horses.

While western stagecoaches flourished until made obsolete by the railroad, they were still considered slow for carrying mail from the central part of the country to the far West. More speed was needed, and the Pony Express was deemed the answer.

The new service, under private ownership, established a 1,966-mile route that began in St. Joseph, Missouri, and ended in Sacramento, California. The goal was to cover it in ten days, cutting fifteen days from the Butterfield Stage's journey.

It was a prodigious undertaking. A total of 190 stations were established at approximately ten-mile intervals. This meant a rider would race at full speed from one station to the next. A fresh horse would be waiting at each stop. Each rider traversed seventy-five miles before being relieved. The first run was made on April 3, 1860.

The horses that pulled the stages were too large for this task. Smaller and faster horses with stamina were needed. The developing western horse, which combined eastern blood from the Thoroughbred with the western Spanish blood, was the answer.

Some 420 horses of this type were purchased and distributed to the stations along the route. About eighty riders were hired to carry the mail.

The Pony Express was a short-lived but exciting endeavor in the country's history. A rider would race through the country, slide to a stop at a pony express station (his horse spent), leap onto the back of a fresh horse, and speed away. Everything possible was done to lighten the horse's load. The riders, for the most part, were light and wiry. Letters were written on thin tissue paper. The saddle and bridle were very light. The riders wore light shoes and clothing and often didn't carry a weapon. Everything was designed for speed.

However, the venture was doomed. Despite having durable, fast horses and good riders, the company was losing money every day despite the five-dollar charge for a half-ounce letter. The last pony express run was made the fall of 1861. The arrival of the telegraph sealed the fate of the Pony Express, as it offered fast, efficient, and cheap communication between the East and West.

Interestingly, some of the eastern horses that went to the far West rebounded east, not as trade or sale animals, but as mounts for the men and women who established sprawling ranches across the western rangelands.

Many of the immigrants who reached Oregon, and even California, discovered that the new land was not paradise. Some who arrived in Oregon, for example, found the high humidity and frequent rainfall not to their liking.

Many of these dispirited journeyers remembered crossing great prairies covered with tall grass. This, they reasoned, would provide excellent grazing for herds of cattle. So, they headed back east, at least as far as the Great Plains, taking their horses with them.

While the Spanish strains and the Thoroughbred formed the nucleus for the early American horse, other strains developed in the East that also later moved west and helped to influence what was to become the western horse of today.

As we look at breeds that influenced the western horse, we can readily see that some resulted from planned breeding programs. Their development shows a continual intermingling of bloodlines to satisfy the needs of the time. Others, such as the Morgan, developed as happenstance.

Arabian

This foundation breed made its way into the United States in the late 1700s. Reportedly, the first Arabian to come to these shores was a stallion named Ranger. He was imported to Connecticut in 1765 and acquired historical fame by siring the horse ridden by General George Washington during the Revolutionary War campaigns.

Continued importations followed, and this classy but durable little horse exerted the influence it started in England all across the United States. One way or another, either through the Thoroughbred or through its own direct connections, its blood shows up in most light-horse breeds.

Morgan

The Morgan is the only breed that traces its lineage to one horse, a foundation sire whose early name was Figure.

Figure was foaled in 1789, and he is believed to be of Thoroughbred and Arabian breeding, though some say the combination was Arabian and Friesian. It is also speculated he might have carried a bit of Welsh blood.

Figure's sire is listed as True Briton, a horse believed to be a Thoroughbred type, whose owner commanded a Tory regiment in Massachusetts during the Revolutionary War. While his owner was drinking at an inn, True Briton, a rather celebrated horse in the area, was reportedly stolen by Yankee patriots and later sold to a farmer near Hartford, Connecticut. The farmer stood True Briton, and one of his offspring was Figure.

Later the farmer made good on an old debt by giving Figure and a gelding to a man named Justin Morgan, whose name would later become the name of the horse. Justin Morgan was a schoolteacher and "singing master." He often traveled from town to town giving singing lessons and establishing choirs. He was not a well man in that he suffered from tuberculosis.

Figure was a dark bay with a refined head — likely the result of Arabian blood — and a solid, compact body. Over short distances, he could out-

run about any horse in the area. He also was a fast trotter and, in addition, could pull more weight than much heavier horses. The stallion lived thirty-two years — from 1789 to 1821 — and sired numerous offspring.

Horses that carried Morgan blood likely helped to carry pioneers west in the waning days of the westward migration. Morgans were horses that could do it all. They could pull a plow, drag logs from the woods, travel far with little rest, run or trot at speed in a race, and pull the family buggy to church on Sunday.

Eventually, these hardy horses were established as a breed in their own right. Through the years they have changed, with the short, stocky look of the old Morgan giving way to horses with a bit more leg and refinement, due in part to show-ring demands.

Horses carrying settlers west likely had Morgan blood.

Standardbred

Today Standardbreds are immediately associated with harness racing. But this wasn't always the case. In the beginning, many Standardbreds were used as carriage horses. When motorized vehicles came along, the breed's concentration became harness racing.

The prime progenitor of the breed was a gray Thoroughbred named Messenger, a descendant of the Darley Arabian. He was imported into the United States in 1789. Messenger was crossed with a mare of Narragansett Pacer blood. The Narragansett Pacer was a road horse of Dutch origin. These horses with a peculiar gait accompanied Dutch settlers to the New World. Their bloodlines influenced the signature gait of the Standardbred pacer as we know it today. However, most of the early Standardbreds were trotters. When a horse trots it moves diagonal legs — left foreleg, right rear leg and right fore, left rear — at the same pace.

One of Messenger's grandsons is considered the foundation sire for the breed, especially the trotters. The horse was Hambletonian, who was foaled in 1849. An estimated ninety percent of all Standardbreds trace to this horse. A poor farmhand named William Rysdyk purchased Hambletonian as a foal along with his dam for $125.

Hambletonian never raced, but reportedly at the age of three, he trotted a mile in 2:48 in a time trial. He was used as a sire from age two until his death at twenty-seven and sired 1,325 offspring. In 1864 he reportedly covered 217 mares. The once-poor Rysdyk earned approximately half a million dollars in breeding fees from Hambletonian.

The name Standardbred eventually was applied to the breed because from 1879 to 1933 eligibility for registration was based on a horse being able to trot the mile in the standard time of 2:30 and to pace it in 2:25.

Standardbred horses have been known for durability and, primarily because of this, their blood has been fused into other breeds.

Missouri Fox Trotter

The Missouri Fox Trotting Horse was developed in the rugged Ozark hills in the nineteenth century. Missouri achieved statehood in 1821, and the first pioneers who settled in the Ozarks came largely from Tennessee, Kentucky, and Virginia.

They brought along horses that had been popular in those areas — such as the American Saddlebred and the Tennessee Walking Horse. These settlers developed what ultimately became the Missouri Fox Trotter by combining Thoroughbred, Arabian, and Morgan blood and later adding crosses of the American Saddlebred and Tennessee Walking Horse. The settlers found that horses that could travel with the easy, broken gait called the Fox Trot were useful and comfortable to ride in the rocky, forest-covered hills of the Ozarks. Soon they were breeding large numbers of these horses for their unique gait. Because of the horse-trading corridor between Missouri and points farther west, a number of Fox Trotters probably accompanied settlers westward.

American Saddlebred

Today's American Saddlebred generally is the peacock of the show ring. However, these horses, too, helped influence the western horse.

The chief progenitor of the breed was Gaines' Denmark, foaled in 1851. He was the son of a Thoroughbred named Denmark, who excelled in four-mile races. The birthplace of the Saddlebred was Kentucky, where breeders combined the blood of English riding horses with that of the Canadian Pacer, Narragansett Pacer, Morgan, Thoroughbred, and Standardbred. The blood of the Narragansett Pacer is thought to help the Saddlebred travel at the ambling gait, which is called the "slow gait" when performed at a leisurely pace and the "rack" when performed at speed.

Saddlebreds became very popular throughout the South. They helped make the cavalry of the South during the Civil War one of the best-mounted units ever to go to war. The breed today can be found across the United States.

Tennessee Walking Horse

Another product of a melting pot of breeds is the Tennessee Walking Horse. The farmers of Tennessee desired an effective utility horse that was also smooth-gaited. Crosses of the Narragansett Pacer, Morgan, Thoroughbred, Standardbred, and American Saddlebred ultimately provided them with a horse that could travel for miles with a smooth, sliding stride. These horses originally were known as "Turn-Rows" because they could travel between rows of crops without damaging them. The Tennessee Walking Horse officially became a breed in 1935. Before that, however, horses of this type spread across the United States.

The Saddlebred has its origins in Kentucky.

The Tennessee Walking Horse developed in the South.

Melting Pot

The horses that graced this country from its early settlement until at least the late 1800s and beyond were the product of different types and strains. In essence, they mirrored what was happening with the population of the United States. Immigrants from many lands were arriving, intermingling, and interbreeding. The country as a whole was a true melting pot of nationalities and cultures and remains so today.

While the human population continued to intermingle and interbreed, specific types of horses became readily identifiable and singled out for breeding programs. Breed registries were created, closing their books to outsiders to maintain and track bloodlines.

Before this occurred, however, an era was ushered in that had a significant impact on the developing western horse.

It was the age of the cowboy.

The Western Horse and the Cowboy

6

To understand the age of the cowboy and the development of his unique horse, we must learn a bit more about the vaqueros of Mexico (known at the time as New Spain). Everything from the cowboy's clothing to his saddle and style of riding can be traced to the vaqueros.

Many of the early Spaniards to arrive in what is now North America were soldiers of fortune in search of gold and silver. However, others recognized that the new land was excellent for raising cattle. Spanish ships conveyed cattle and horses.

The Spaniards introduced three strains of cattle: the Berenda, which was black and white; the Retinto, which was cherry red to tan; and the ganado prieto, which produced the black fighting bulls of Spain.

Many of the Spanish cattle weren't branded. Eventually, disputes arose among the Spaniards over both land and cattle ownership. To prevent these disputes from worsening, Spanish authorities in Mexico City established the first stockmen's association in the Americas in 1529, only ten years after Cortez and his soldiers had arrived in the New World.

Called the Mesta, the association set rules and a procedure for enforcing them among the cattlemen. One of the first rules was that each stockman must brand all of his livestock. Each brand had to be registered, thus establishing the continent's first brand book.

The grazing areas for the burgeoning cattle population continued to expand, sometimes at the expense of small farms where natives tilled the soil. Eventually the Spanish crown set up a huge communal grazing tract north and west of Mexico City.

As the herds continued to multiply, the Spaniards needed someone to control the cattle's movements and to gather and brand them. They also needed someone to prevent the frequent thievery. The job

Chaps evolved out of necessity.

fell to what became the first cowboys.

The early Mexican cowboy has never been as revered as his subsequent American counterpart. The Spanish landowners looked on tending cattle as common work. They saw no romance to it. As a result, the first cowboys often were poor natives, blacks, and other non-Spaniards.

The first vaqueros were taught to ride a horse and to tend the cattle. They adopted a style of dress unique to their vocation.

Working all day in the hot sun, for example, required shade or protection. This gave birth to the sombrero, with its low, flat crown and wide, stiff brim. Later, the cowboy of the West would make modifications better suited to windy conditions. These cowboys needed something smaller, and the "cowboy hat" came into being.

The vaquero often had to ride through brush. To protect his legs, he wore leather pants, the precursor to chaps. Often the leather pants were held in place by a colorful sash, which he used during the winter to keep his midsection warm. In the beginning many vaqueros went barefoot, especially in the warmer regions, though some likely had boots handed down by their Spanish masters. Almost all wore spurs, even if they had to be strapped to bare ankles.

The horses that carried these early cowboys were descendants of the horses shipped from Spain. Because the Spanish believed that gelding a horse diminished its strength and that mares were inferior, most of the vaqueros rode stallions.

Eventually, the vaqueros became responsible for rounding up the cattle that roamed freely across huge communal grazing land and driving them to holding areas where the calves could be branded and those animals selected for slaughter could be pulled.

The first vaqueros rode in saddles brought over from Spain by the Conquistadors. The saddles were heavy and cumbersome, suited for an armored soldier and not a vaquero. The pommel (the head or front of the saddle) and cantle (the rear bow of the saddle) wrapped around the rider. It was designed to keep the armored soldier, who would be helpless on the ground, in the saddle as he did battle with lance and sword against his enemies. The stirrups were quite short, something that made for uncomfortable long rides, as well as poor balance.

The vaquero modified the saddle. He made it less confining, lengthening the stirrups for better balance and more comfort. Later, when the vaquero began using a lariat to catch and hold cattle, the saddle horn was enlarged and strengthened. The early American cowboy used the same type of saddle as the vaquero, but when the big cattle drives began in the 1860s, the western saddle as we know it today evolved.

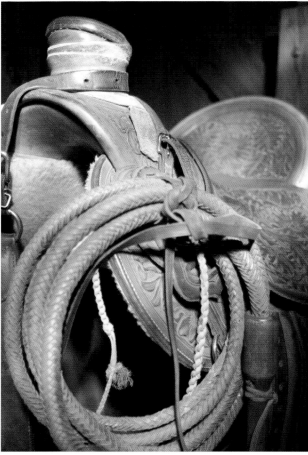

The western saddles of today have their origins in the ones used by vaqueros.

The early vaquero's equipment did not include a lariat or lasso. Instead, the vaquero used a long, iron-tipped lance to separate cattle or prod them along.

To kill the cattle more efficiently for their hides, the vaqueros fashioned a curved steel blade, somewhat like a scythe, and fastened it to a stout pole about ten to twelve feet long.

He would ride up behind a cow and jam the sharp blade against the large tendon in a rear leg, severing it and crippling the animal. The vaquero would then dismount and drive the same sharp blade into the animal's head just behind the horns, killing it. The hide would be skinned, the tallow removed, and the rest of the carcass left behind.

The slaughter of thousands of cattle for tallow and hides substantially decreased the bovine population in Mexico for a time. Eventually, the hamstringing weapon was outlawed. The vaquero decided that a rope would serve his purposes better than the lance for capturing cattle, but in the interim he combined the two. A loop was placed on the end of a lance and the vaquero would ride up and drop this over the animal's horns.

Later, the lance was cast aside for just the lariat. Next, the vaquero learned to twirl the lariat over his head and throw it with accuracy. The first lariats were likely braided from strips of untanned cowhide and tied either to the cinch on the saddle or to a horse's tail. Both methods were inhumane and not very effective. The need for a better base led to the stronger, larger saddle horn.

While we like to think that trail drives are unique to the western cowboy, they actually originated in Mexico. As ranches spread farther north, the prime market for beef remained in the more densely populated Mexico City area. The vaqueros would gather and drive the cattle from the sparsely populated ranches southward to market.

The Spaniards did not castrate bull calves, making the herd more difficult to manage. To control the bulls, the vaqueros would rope some of the bulls and, with a rope and halter, tie them to trained oxen. The oxen would drag the bulls until they were broken to lead and learned to submit. The bulls were then released and often became the herd leaders on the trail. The lead bulls were precursors to the trained lead steers that one day would set the course for the cattle herds driven across the United States.

The vaqueros of Mexico eventually became skilled horsemen and ropers. They developed their own culture, with fathers passing the skills to their sons.

Early cowboys adapted their equipment and cowboy hats from those of the vaquero.

Eventually, the cattle herds of Mexico spread north and west into what is now Texas and California. With the cattle went the vaquero, his horse, and his lariat. In California, the vaqueros became excellent horsemen, developing unique training techniques that are still used. For example, the hackamore (a bitless bridle), or bosal, as it is often called today, was developed in California.

The California vaquero wouldn't train a horse until it was at least three years old, and for the first few years of its training, a horse would be ridden using the hackamore or bosal. The theory was that a hackamore preserved a soft mouth in the horse, making the animal easier to control when the bit was introduced after training.

California's mild climate allowed the vaqueros to hone their skills year round. Stories are told of vaqueros roping grizzly bears for sport, with a couple of vaqueros roping the front legs and a couple roping the rear legs. The animal then was stretched between the teams.

Most ranches raised their own horses, with the mares running wild in bands, and each band being serviced by a selected stallion. When the vaqueros needed replacement horses, they rounded up the band and cut out and roped their choices.

As herds expanded, the vaquero kept moving north. Soon, he met American settlers drifting south.

Connecticut native Moses Austin, who had established mining settlements in Missouri, had approached the Spanish governor in San Antonio in 1820 about allowing American citizens to settle in the Texas territory. Austin was seeking a way to turn his business fortunes around after the banking panic of 1819. On the trip home, he contracted pneumonia and died shortly after returning to Missouri, but not before entreating his son, twenty-seven-year-old Stephen, to complete the venture.

Ultimately, Stephen F. Austin negotiated an agreement with the new government of Mexico that allowed thousands of Americans to immigrate. Many

of them had fallen on hard times and were looking for a new start. They could get it in Texas, where land could be obtained almost for free.

The colonists came from many parts of America, bringing along their horses and cattle. Because many of the new settlers came from places like Kentucky and Tennessee, their horses reflected breeding programs in those areas. Many of the horses had some Chickasaw and Thoroughbred-type blood.

That is not to say that all horses or even the majority were Chickasaw-Thoroughbred crosses. Rather, many of the horses on which the colonists arrived were a hodgepodge of types and bloodlines. The prime criterion was that they be a "saddle horse," one that could be ridden. This ruled out draft blood but not much else. We can assume that Morgan, Arabian, and Missouri Fox Trotter blood also flowed in the veins of some of the arriving equines.

In many instances the arriving settlers handled cattle very differently than ranchers in Mexico and California. In the northern and mid-western states, men and boys on foot herded most cattle, so they had little in common with vaqueros, who did almost everything from horseback.

The new arrivals from southern states better understood Mexican cattle ranching. The Southerners raised more cattle than did their counterparts farther north and handled a good deal of stock on horseback.

The settlers that arrived in Texas in the mid- and late 1820s were more interested in obtaining land for farming than in cattle ranching. However, some of the newcomers brought cattle with them and quickly realized that much of Texas was better suited to raising grass for cattle to graze than for raising crops. At this time, Texas was part of a Mexican state called Coahuila y Tejas that combined the Texas territory and the Mexican state of Coahuila, which borders Texas along the Big Bend stretch of the Rio Grande.

Cattle brought in by the colonists were soon mixing with Spanish cattle that had drifted north into the Texas territory and were now running wild. Spanish missionaries who left Mexico after its independence from Spain in 1821 had abandoned their herds. Others cattle strayed from Mexican ranches. The intermingling soon produced an animal that ultimately would become the Texas longhorn, a hardy breed.

The longhorns' color patterns ranged widely, but one thing was consistent — they all had long pointed horns. They were tall, long-legged, hardy animals with bodies that were long and narrow. They were able to cover a lot of ground quickly and could subsist on whatever vegetation existed in their locale. Longhorn cows proved to be excellent progenitors, giving birth to small calves that grew rapidly. However, longhorns were, for the most part, still wild and difficult to handle.

As cattle operations grew in size and number in the 1830s, Americans looked to the Mexican vaquero for help and information about raising cattle and training horses. While the Americans learned how

vaqueros handled horses and cattle, the vaqueros found a new market for wild horses, which they captured and sold to the Americans.

The vaqueros constructed holding corrals into which they drove the wild bands. This method of capture let them cull the less desirable horses and keep only the elite for sale.

Eventually, the Texians, as the American settlers came to be called, captured their own horses in the wild and tamed them. They soon discovered, however, that their eastern saddles were not appropriate for roping or working stock, and they quickly adopted the vaqueros' saddle.

The American colonists and the Mexican government were destined to collide. About six years after passing the immigration law of 1824 that opened the floodgates for Americans into Texas, the Mexican government sought to stop the influx. The Texians immediately objected and, eventually, a revolution ensued. It ended with the Republic of Texas coming into existence in 1836.

Part of a cowboy's job was to round up strays and bring them back to the herd.

During the revolution some of the Texians formed raiding parties that went into what is now Mexico and drove herds of cattle back into Texas, either for slaughter or for sale as seedstock.

As the Texas herds outgrew the local need for beef, markets were sought elsewhere. In the 1840s Texas ranchers began trailing herds of cattle to New Orleans, where the animals could be sold for a profit.

The men who tended the cattle in Texas and drove them to market were first referred to as cowboys about this time, but it wasn't until the 1860s that the term, helped by pulp-fiction writers, really caught on and "drover" was forever replaced by "cowboy."

Learning from the vaquero, the Texas cowboy became adept at handling a rope, capturing and breaking horses, and working cattle from horseback.

The type of horse he preferred was also changing. An interest in sprint racing had prompted more horses from the South and East to be brought to Texas by newcomers from places like Tennessee,

Ohio, Illinois, and Kentucky. Two significant sires were Steel Dust, foaled in 1843 and brought to Texas as a yearling, and Shiloh, foaled in 1844 and brought to Texas in 1849. Both were outstanding sprinters and were used extensively at stud. Their bloodlines, along with those of other similar horses, were shaping a powerful and agile sprinter. It wasn't long before cowboys of that era discovered this new breed of horse was adept at working cattle.

Unfortunately, the market for Texas cattle was limited. The state was sparsely populated, and only so many animals could be sold through New Orleans and other southern markets. There was a demand for beef in the North but no practical way to get the cattle there.

Then the Civil War began in 1861.

The war produced an immediate need for Texas cattle and a number of herds were trailed east to provide beef for the Confederate army. Before long, however, Union forces and a blockade of southern ports

Longhorn cattle could be difficult to handle on the early drives.

cut off that market and Texas cattle remained home.

When the Civil War began, many Texas cattlemen, young and old, rallied to the Confederate cause and went off to war. Women, young boys, and old men took over cattle ranching. It was not a pleasant life. Help was short and drought hit the state during three of the war years, followed by bitterly cold winters. As a result, cattle were widely spread, breeding indiscriminately as they roamed the countryside.

With the war's end in 1865, Texas cattlemen returned home, but the homecoming wasn't particularly glorious. The state's economy was in a deplorable condition, and their cattle, many of them unbranded, were scattered over thousands of acres of countryside.

This necessitated a cattle roundup, called a cow hunt. Ranchers and cowboys headed into the bush country where they would round up errant cattle, rope and brand the calves, and then herd them back to their respective ranches. The roundups continued for some years because fences were few, making it impossible to keep cattle from drifting.

Roundups took place in the spring and fall and were communal efforts. Each participating ranch sent a group of cowboys to one central location. The cowboys would start each day from there and spread out through the countryside "riding circle," which means they rode a long, circular route and drove all the cattle they found to the central location. Once the cattle were gathered into a large group, the cowboys would cut out the calves and brand them with the same brand the mother was carrying, if she had been branded. Calves from unbranded mothers, we can assume, were divided among the ranchers.

During these roundups, the cowboys began noticing certain horses had specific talents or characteristics, traits that were later bred for. Some horses, for instance, could quietly enter a herd and push out a cow and calf without disturbing the rest. Others proved to be steady mounts for roping, tying, and dragging calves to the branding fire. Still others — and they

were highly valued — were excellent "night horses."

Without fences or corrals on the open range in Texas, the cattle were kept in a loosely held group until the sorting and branding were finished.

At night the cowboys took turns riding around the herd and keeping the cattle from drifting. The night watch also kept the cattle relaxed and quiet. A prancing, whinnying horse wouldn't do. Nor would one with poor eyesight. Though horses have much better night vision than humans, those with superior night vision, plus a quiet temperament, were ideal.

Once the cattle had been gathered, sorted, and branded, the outfits would move to another part of the open range and repeat the process. Eventually each outfit would trail toward home, driving the cattle that had been selected for market, with the rest returning to the open range.

The market lay in the North, where during the war the Union army had eaten its way through the local stock. More beef was needed, but getting the longhorns there was a problem because Texas had no rail lines.

Charles Goodnight, a former freighter and Texas Ranger, had an answer: trail the cattle to points where they could be loaded onto railroad cars or sold.

Goodnight had turned to raising cattle in 1856, when some five million longhorns were spread across Texas, many of them unbranded. At about the time Goodnight was becoming heavily involved in the cattle business, famed army scout Kit Carson was leading troops against the Navajos in New Mexico. The troops rounded up some seven thousand Navajos and placed them on a reservation. The Navajos and the soldiers guarding them would need beef, Goodnight reasoned. In the wake of the Civil War, Goodnight, who was in his early thirties, met Oliver Loving, a trail driver in his fifties who had already herded cattle north to Illinois and Denver. The two joined forces, and in 1866, with a group of cowboys, started two thousand head of longhorns across Texas to New Mexico. It was an arduous trip because they had to travel ninety-six miles across the Staked Plains (Llano Estacado), where there was no water. Many Native Americans lived along the route and posed a constant threat.

Despite the hardships, the drive concluded successfully. Loving also took stock cows and bulls farther north to Denver and Cheyenne, and the route from Texas north became known as the Goodnight-Loving Trail. In 1867 Loving was killed by Comanches along the trail he had helped establish. Goodnight went on to amass a fortune in the cattle business, and at his peak, he was running one hundred thousand head of cattle on nearly one million acres. He crossed longhorns with Shorthorns and Herefords, which did much to upgrade the quality of his herd.

Cattlemen in eastern Texas also were seeking markets for their animals. Some tried to drive herds to Illinois, but irate farmers in Missouri barred their way, fearing the cattle would trample their crops and spread disease.

An entrepreneur named Joseph McCoy, an Illinois meat dealer, decided to instead drive the cattle to a railhead a little farther west. He settled on Abilene, Kansas, a drowsy little railhead on the Plains. McCoy bought some acreage around the tiny community, which had good grass and good water. He built holding pens for the cattle and then spread the word that Abilene was the place to end a cattle drive. That first year alone — 1867 — some 35,000 head of cattle arrived at the railhead. In 1868 that number had swelled to 75,000.

Cowboys drove the cattle north along a trail from the Red River that a half-Cherokee, half-white man named Jesse Chisholm had taken two years earlier. It has been estimated that between 1869 and 1871 nearly a million and a half Texas cattle arrived in Abilene, many of them making the trek on the Chisholm Trail.

Other Kansas railheads also became shipping centers, and towns like Dodge City, Ellsworth, Newton, and Wichita became rip-roaring cattle towns.

Driving cattle from Texas to the cow towns was time consuming. It took about three months to travel from San Antonio to Abilene. It could also be dangerous. A thunderstorm might incite a stampede, with cattle tossing their horns and racing along wildly, trampling everything in their path. Then, too, disaster could strike in a moment while crossing rivers, some swollen by heavy rains. It is no wonder that a dependable horse was highly valued.

The cowboy's horse had to be versatile to withstand the rigors of cattle drives. It had to have the speed to dash after a herd "quitter" and turn it back toward the group. It had to have the courage to plunge into a swollen stream and swim to the other side. It had to have the stamina to walk hour after hour, day after day, with grass its only sustenance. It had to have good feet and good legs to withstand the constant travel and still remain sound.

Not just any mount would do when a man had to depend on the horse for his safety and very life on a trail drive.

During the first few days of the drive, cattle were pushed along as many as twenty-five miles a day, as the cowboys sought to get them far enough away from home so they wouldn't turn back. Once that was accomplished, they usually traveled eight to ten miles per day. Of course, available grass and water had a strong bearing on how far they pushed each day. The cattle were allowed to graze as they moved along. The goal was to arrive at a watering spot at night with the cattle tired, but with full stomachs.

The cowboys would then bend the long line of cattle around until they were milling in a large group. If all went well, the cattle were plenty willing to stop, drink, and bed down for the night.

That is, unless something spooked them.

The night watch had to make certain the cattle remained bedded down, calm, and content. Cowboys often sang softly as they rode, something the western movies would pick up on later. Only, in the movies the celluloid cowboy often played guitar and sang to a pretty girl. The cowboy on the trail didn't have a guitar, and his singing served a practical purpose.

The first watch normally would run until ten o' clock; the second watch would be from ten o' clock until midnight; the third from midnight until two o' clock in the morning; and the final watch from two o' clock until daybreak.

When morning dawned, the cook would serve the cowboys breakfast and the cattle would be roused and started down the trail again. The trail boss normally would ride in front, showing the way. The cook and the chuck wagon would follow. Two "point" riders behind them kept the leaders of the herd moving in the right direction. Next were two "swing" riders, one on each side of the herd. Behind them were two "flank" riders, also one on each side of the herd. Pushing along the stragglers would be three or four "drag" riders. The remuda — the cowboys' extra horses — would run parallel with the front of the cattle herd.

Cattle drives became more challenging as they continued north, all the way to Montana and Wyoming, a trip that could last six months. The gold rush of 1862 had resulted in thousands of fortune-seekers flocking to the area, prompting the first cattle drives to Montana.

Other cattle drives into the high plains country would follow, thus bringing the Texas cowboy culture and its horses into a new region.

The cowboys who trailed the herds north were young, on the average about twenty-four, and came from diverse backgrounds. One man, Teddy Blue, would write about life on the trail in his book, *We Pointed Them North*. Blue was born in England and brought to Nebraska as a young boy. He was frail, but his father allowed him to accompany a trail drive

Cowboys needed calm, reliable horses for long cattle drives or roundups.

when the boy was only ten. The father reasoned that living outdoors for a time would improve Teddy's health. That experience turned Teddy Blue into a confirmed cowboy. The lad made his first drive north in 1871 and his last one in 1883 when he was but twenty-four. Teddy Blue, like many of the cowboys, was slight of stature, it being reasoned that large, heavy men were too hard on a horse. Originally the cowboys' horse was slight of stature as well, but underwent a transformation through the mid 1800s.

In Texas, the breeding of stocky sprint-type horses that looked like Steel Dust and Shiloh had contin-

Cowboys remain a necessity on cattle ranches.

ued through the Civil War. When the trail drives headed north, cowboys sought this type of horse. Thus, the cattle drives helped spread the bloodlines and the horses with certain physical characteristics that we have come to call the western horse.

While historians have adequately documented

the Texas cowboys and their cattle drives, not as much has been said about those drives that moved west to east. Many who settled in Oregon went into the cattle business. Thanks to a long growing season and good grass, the cattle flourished. Before long, supply also exceeded demand there, and cattlemen began looking for new outlets. They concentrated on Montana and Idaho and drove their cattle there in the same manner as the Texans.

Inevitably many of the new arrivals from Texas and Oregon took a long look at the sprawling prairies of grass in Wyoming, Montana, and the Dakotas and decided these areas would be prime country for raising cattle.

Soon cattle roamed over giant expanses of open range on the western plains, with cowboys still applying their skills on horseback. By the 1880s, however, barbed wire fences ended the days of the open range, and the railroads dipping into Texas made trail drives unnecessary.

Thus, the heyday of the cowboy ended, but he and his horse still remained a necessity on the fenced-in ranches. There were still cattle to be rounded up, even though they were confined, and there were calves to be sorted, roped, and branded. The cowboy would continue to rely on a good horse as his ally and more and more care and planning would be exercised to develop the ideal western horse.

The Quarter Horse

The American Quarter Horse typifies the western horse. It also happens to be the most popular breed in the United States — more than four million Quarter Horses have been registered with the American Quarter Horse Association, which boasts a membership well in excess of 300,000.

While Quarter Horses have been around a long time, the registry has not. A group of horsemen and ranchers from the Southwest founded the registry in 1940 to preserve pedigrees of ranch horses whose lineage traced to the early 1600s.

The Quarter Horse as we know it today — a muscular but extremely agile, durable horse with strong bones and a calm temperament — evolved primarily in Texas, Oklahoma, New Mexico, eastern Colorado, and Kansas. Ranchers in these states bred horses for their ability to work cattle and win sprint races.

However, the hardy Chickasaw pony, descendant of Spanish imports that colonists obtained from Native Americans, is the true foundation of the Quarter Horse breed. Through the years, Chickasaw ponies were bred with Thoroughbreds and other horses, resulting in the versatile Quarter Horse. The

Chickasaw also was versatile, often serving as riding horse, work horse, and racehorse.

The colonists quickly discovered that their hardy

The agility of the modern Quarter Horse is a hallmark of the breed.

little animals could leap into a gallop from a standstill and sprint with blazing speed for a quarter of a mile or so. Sprint races caught on fast, often with a great deal of money wagered on the outcome.

The horses raced on small-town streets or in abandoned fields, a far cry from today's cushiony track surfaces. The horse had to be surefooted and swift to survive, let alone win, one of these races.

As more Thoroughbred-type horses were imported from England, sprint racing lost its appeal in some areas, particularly along the Atlantic seaboard, and was replaced by longer races ultimately run on oval tracks.

Those first oval tracks often were as crude as the makeshift short tracks. Sometimes they were simply staked out with poles in large, open fields. The horses would run around the outside of the poles. The ground was usually uneven and bumpy, maybe even containing old tree stumps. The first recorded race meet under these conditions was run over a three-mile course in Hanover County, Virginia, in 1737.

Growing interest in distance racing led to the importation of a stallion, Janus, from England in the mid-1750s. Though he was imported to sire distance horses, Janus became a significant sire for the Quarter Horse breed. His offspring and their descendants were often excellent sprinters.

A grandson of the Godolphin Arabian, Janus had been a successful racehorse in England, twice winning impressively in four-mile heats. An injury forced his retirement, and he stood at stud until Mordecai Booth, a wealthy American plantation and ship owner, bought him and took him home to Gloucester, Virginia.

Janus was not large, standing just a little taller than fourteen hands, but he reportedly had excellent conformation, and, as it would turn out, possessed the right genes to become a sire of significance. His good qualities so overshadowed the bad, genetically, that he was often inbred, siring foals from daughters and granddaughters that inherited his positive qualities.

After arriving in America, Janus recovered from his injury, and Mordecai put him back on the track. He ran the stallion in four-mile heats, where Janus proved he not only had speed but durability as well.

The early distance horses in both England and America were built like Janus, rather than tall, lanky Thoroughbred types. As the Thoroughbred became taller, lighter boned, and faster, but with less stamina, races of a mile or less replaced heat racing.

Janus was later retired to stud in southern Virginia and North Carolina, where sprint races had retained their popularity. He soon attained a reputation for siring horses that were great sprinters. However, when he bred mares that were distance runners, he begat distance runners.

Sons of his, such as Twigg, Old Peacock, Meade's Celer, and Babram, along with a grandson named Bacchus, carried on the Janus tradition of siring fast sprinters. The daughters of Janus, on the other hand, had a strong influence on the Thoroughbred breed because they tended to produce distance horses.

As mentioned earlier, Janus and his offspring were not large. Janus was listed as being fourteen hands, three quarters of an inch, while Twig measured fourteen hands, one inch.

Babram, a son of Janus, was known as the fastest short-distance horse of his day. He also had a lengthy career. He died at age twenty-three in 1789 during a race in Mecklenburg County, Virginia. He was running against Juniper, also a son of Janus, and was well ahead when he stumbled, fell, and broke his neck.

Oval racing eventually doomed sprint racing along the Atlantic Seaboard. As sprint racing moved inland, so did the equine line that would become Quarter Horses. Kentucky, Tennessee, Missouri, Ohio, Michigan, and Illinois became the new breeding centers. From these states, the Quarter Horse of that day made its way into Kansas, Oklahoma, and Texas, where its popularity grew.

Flimnap, another imported stallion of the Janus

era, was very popular in the Carolinas. Like Janus, he was a grandson of the Godolphin Arabian. When bred to the stout Chickasaw mares, he sired sprinters with speed, and when bred to Thoroughbred types, he sired horses that could stay the course for distance races. He stood fourteen hands, one inch.

Flimnap had already established his reputation as a sire when the Revolutionary War began. So great was his reputation that the British were determined to capture the eleven-year-old stallion, who was owned by Major Isaac C. Harleston. Harleston was serving under General Nathanael Greene in the Continental Army.

Lord Cornwallis, who commanded British troops in the South, established his headquarters very near Harleston's plantation. Periodically, he would launch a raid in an attempt to capture Flimnap and some of the other well-bred horses on the plantation. However, spies would sound the alarm, and the horses would be spirited off into the swamps before the British troops arrived.

Finally, the British resorted to harsher tactics. They captured one of the plantation's stable boys and tried to force him to tell them where the horses were hidden. The stable boy refused, and the British decided to hang him. They rode off and left the lad dangling from a tree limb. A companion who was hiding nearby cut him down, still alive.

Later, the British organized another raid on the Harleston plantation. However, the Continentals intercepted them, causing the British to retreat, empty-handed.

The British made yet another attempt to steal Flimnap. An ill-tempered Scot named "Crazy" Campbell commanded the contingent that had been turned back by the Continentals. Infuriated at being thwarted, he put together a more powerful force and vowed to burn the Harleston plantation to the ground.

As Campbell rode up to the plantation with his troop, a young belle, whom he had met in Charleston while she was visiting relatives sympathetic to the crown, marched out to meet him and invited him inside. Surprised and flattered, Campbell ordered the troops to refrain from the pillaging and burning that had been planned. When he left, the premises were unharmed and Flimnap undisturbed. Flimnap lived out his twenty-six years at the Harleston plantation, siring a number of quality foals.

Sir Archy, a big Thoroughbred, followed Janus as a strong sire for the Quarter Horse breed. At the outset he appeared an unlikely breeding candidate because, unlike the smaller Janus, he stood at sixteen hands.

Sir Archy, foaled in 1805, was a son of the Thoroughbred sire Diomed, who had been imported to Virginia at age twenty-one in 1798. Sir Archy showed power and substance on his sixteen-hand frame. He didn't race often. However, when he did run, he normally won.

With his lineage tracing to the Byerley Turk through Herod, Sir Archy and his offspring dominated from 1800 to 1850 in the breeding of what would become Quarter Horses, just as Janus and his offspring had dominated from 1752 to 1800.

Sir Archy's son Copper Bottom also made his mark as a sire. Foaled in 1828, he was taken to Texas in 1839 by General Sam Houston. Copper Bottom lived until 1860 and sired many foals in the Galveston area.

Beginning with the first importations in the mid-1700s, Thoroughbreds or Thoroughbred types continually added their blood to what became the Quarter Horse breed. Eighteen sires out of the first nineteen in Volume I of the *American Quarter Horse Stud Book* carried in excess of fifty percent Thoroughbred blood, and only a very few in that first listing did not carry at least some immediate Thoroughbred breeding in their pedigrees.

In the mid-1800s the yet-unnamed breed, which was still in the "budding" stage, produced some top-quality stallions that profoundly influenced the Quarter Horse.

As mentioned in Chapter 6, Steel Dust was one of those stallions. In fact, his role was so integral that for years many old-timers referred to Quarter Horse types simply as "Steel Dusts."

Steel Dust was foaled in 1843 in either Illinois or Kentucky — there are two accounts as to his birthplace. His lineage traces to Sir Archy. Steel Dust was sired by Harry Bluff, a son of Short Whip. Steel Dust's dam was a Thoroughbred named Big Nance. She was by Timoleon, a son of Sir Archy.

Steel Dust, acquired as a yearling by Texans Middleton Perry and Jones Greene, matured into a stallion that stood a little more than fifteen hands and weighed about 1,200 pounds.

The owners of the handsome bay stallion decided to test his mettle in match races. He outran even the fastest horses in the area. One of Steel Dust's most notable races came in 1855 against Kentucky-bred Monmouth, who was based in McKinney, Texas, on the north side of Dallas. Almost nothing is known about Monmouth and his breeding other than he was a sprinter with blazing speed who had won many races in Kentucky before moving to Texas. There is speculation that he traced back to the imported Whip, whose lineage went back to Herod.

Everyone wanted to attend this racing event of the year, and even the courts closed down.

So many people showed up in McKinney for the race that the town's hotel reportedly was turned over to the ladies, and the men slept wherever they could find space.

Although Monmouth was the hometown favorite, Steel Dust solidified his reputation as the fastest horse in those parts by defeating him and providing a big payday for his backers in the heavily bet race.

Later that summer, prominent Texas horse breeder Jack Batchler agreed to race his Shiloh against Steel Dust. Shiloh, like Steel Dust, was a blazing fast sprinter with a widespread reputation. He had been sired by Van Tromp and traced back to Sir Archy. Foaled at Batchler's Tennessee farm in 1844, Shiloh accompanied Batchler when he moved his family and horses to Texas a year later.

In Texas, Batchler lived near Middleton Perry, and the two men became good friends, which might explain why they had never before raced their stallions against each other.

The match race between the stellar stallions was to be held near Dallas, at one of the best short tracks in the racing world. A few thousand people lived in Dallas at the time, and they loved racing. The track was ahead of its day, featuring chutes as a starting gate and a

The early days of Quarter Horse racing helped shape the breed.

quarter-mile straightaway that was free of rocks, stumps, and other obstructions. As the horses awaited the start, Steel Dust reared up against the starting chute. One of the boards broke and rammed his shoulder, puncturing it. Steel Dust never raced again.

When he died in the late 1860s, he left dozens of sons and daughters that were fleet and excellent in conformation. His descendants became outstanding cattle-working horses and, later, fierce competitors.

Some of Steel Dust's greatest foals were out of daughters of Shiloh.

Shiloh's reputation as a stallion grew during his racing and stud careers, and many mares were booked to him. Unfortunately his owner often failed to record the name or pedigree of the mare bred, just the name of her owner. Shiloh lived to age thirty.

One of Shiloh's offspring, Old Billy, who was out of Ram Cat, by Steel Dust, strongly influenced the evolution of the Quarter Horse. While some old timers called the Quarter Horses of those years "Steel Dusts," others called them "Billys."

Old Billy's early life as a stallion left a lot to be desired. His original owner left his Texas farm to fight in the Civil War. While the owner was gone, his wife fed and watered Billy, but kept him chained to the tree where her husband had left him. At the war's conclusion, Billy was purchased by William B. "Billy" Fleming, who had returned to Texas after fighting in the Civil War.

Billy was in terrible condition when Fleming purchased him. The chain around his neck had left a distinct scar, and his hooves were so long they had to be sawed off. Once the horse recovered, however, he turned into a superb breeding stallion whose offspring served as cornerstones of the emerging breed.

A son of Steel Dust also influenced the look and type of the emerging breed. His name was Cold Deck. Like so many of those early horses, his history includes an interesting tale.

Steel Dust's owner decreed he must be present whenever the stallion covered a mare and that Steel Dust shouldn't be bred during his racing seasons. During one race meet, Steel Dust was left in the care of a groom while the owner was elsewhere. The groom, the story goes, got into a poker game and lost all of his money. One of the poker players had a mare he wanted to breed to Steel Dust, and he cajoled the now-penniless groom into continuing the game with a breeding to Steel Dust as a stake. The groom agreed, and then lost again. A secretive breeding took place, and the mare became pregnant. The resulting foal would fittingly be called Cold Deck.

No one knows whether the story is fact, but the fifteen-hand sorrel Cold Deck made some serious waves in the local racing community and later in the breeding shed.

The blood of Steel Dust and Shiloh ran through the veins of another "impact" stallion. Dan Tucker was foaled in 1887, sired by Barney Owens, a Cold Deck son.

Dan Tucker was powerfully built, standing fifteen hands and weighing about 1,300 pounds. He began racing as a two-year-old. His most famous race was against The Sheriff, a horse by the same sire. The Sheriff had been purchased in Illinois, where Dan Tucker was born. He had had great success racing in north Texas, Kansas, Illinois, and Missouri.

Dan Tucker and The Sheriff met up in St. Louis in the early 1890s over a 440-yard course. Dan Tucker won the race in a sizzling :22 flat, a new record on a Missouri track.

When he retired from the track, Dan Tucker was put to stud and proved as excellent a sire as he was a racehorse. He sired a great many noteworthy offspring, but none greater than Peter McCue, foaled in 1895.

Robert Denhardt, one of the founding fathers of the AQHA and a noted historian for the breed, had this to say about Peter McCue in his book, *Quarter Horses*:

"Peter McCue's blood had greater influence on the development of the Quarter Horse between 1900 and 1940 than that of any other individual. His sons were in demand and were scattered among all of the principal Quarter Horse areas. For example, Hickory Bill in south Texas; Harmon Baker in central Texas, and John Wilkins in north Texas. The same was true in other states like Colorado, New Mexico and Oklahoma, where offspring of Peter McCue were found out-running, out-performing and out-producing all rivals."

Peter McCue stood sixteen hands and in his prime weighed 1,430 pounds. He first grabbed attention as a gifted sprinter, winning races in Texas, Oklahoma, and Illinois.

Stories are told about his extraordinary speed. During one morning workout, three clockers timed him in :21 for 440 yards. The time would have been a record, but because it occurred during a workout, it wasn't official.

Peter McCue died in 1923 at age twenty-eight. So influential and popular was this stallion's bloodline that by January 1, 1948, AQHA records revealed that of the 11,510 Quarter Horses registered, 2,304 of them traced in male line to Peter McCue.

The divergent bloodlines that became the Quarter Horse were well represented in Joe Hancock, a grandson of Peter McCue. Foaled in 1923, Joe Hancock was sired by John Wilkins, whose dam was a Thoroughbred mare named Kate Wawekas.

Joe Hancock's dam was known simply as the Hancock mare. She was sired by a horse named Ralph Wilson, a compact, black Percheron. The dam of the Hancock mare was known as the Mundell mare and was described as being of Steel Dust lineage.

Thus, in the pedigree of Joe Hancock, who was later inducted into the AQHA Hall of Fame, we have Thoroughbred, draft horse, and sprinter blood, the latter coming from Steel Dust via Peter McCue.

Joe Hancock, who was described as being well proportioned and well balanced and about the same size as Peter McCue, was an excellent racehorse, but today he is better known as an influential stallion

whose descendants are favored by many ropers for their size, strength, and durability.

Many of Peter McCue's offspring became outstanding performance horses, racers, sires, and dams. One of his descendants, in fact, helped mold both the look and performance of the Quarter Horse and, thus, the western horse.

That horse would ultimately be registered as Old Sorrel. Foaled in 1915, he was by Hickory Bill, one of the top-flight sons of Peter McCue, and his dam was a Thoroughbred owned by George Clegg, a prominent breeder for some fifty years.

The story of Old Sorrel's life and accomplishments revolves around the famous King Ranch in south Texas and the members of the Kleberg family who operate it. The sprawling ranch concentrated on raising cattle and horses. It was so huge that hundreds of saddle horses were required for the cowboys and vaqueros working there.

Robert Kleberg Jr. ran the horse operation. In his mind, he faced a dilemma. He didn't think that the Thoroughbred had enough cow sense to fill the bill for ranch work. At the same time, he thought that the more compact horses that many of his cowboys and vaqueros were riding were too short and muscular for all-around use. He wanted something in between.

Caesar Kleberg, a cousin who ran one of the divisions of the ranch, agreed with Bob, and when he saw Old Sorrel, then a six-month-old colt, at George Clegg's place, he felt that the search for a foundation stallion was over. In the beginning the horse carried the name of his breeder, George Clegg, but as time went by, the vaqueros at the ranch gave him a Spanish name, which translated into "The Old Sorrel."

Before putting the horse into their breeding program, the Klebergs tried him as a saddle horse. Old Sorrel demonstrated uncommon cow savvy and was fast and agile. Robert Kleberg had his ideal cowhorse.

Kleberg began a sophisticated and dedicated breeding program. He was no amateur. After all, he had masterminded a new breed of cattle that were ideally suited for that arid part of Texas — the Santa Gertrudis.

There was more to the breeding program than putting a group of mares to Old Sorrel. It started that way, but then came the distilling. The bottom half of each colt crop was immediately gelded and placed in the general saddle horse band. Horses comprising the top half, based on conformation and ability, were trained and ridden by family members and the top hands on the ranch.

The riders and Kleberg would then rank the horses according to their capabilities. Only the best were kept as stallions and broodmares. Kleberg also didn't hesitate to concentrate Old Sorrel's blood through inbreeding. Denhardt reports that when the Quarter Horse Registry was formed in 1940, eight sons and grandsons of Old Sorrel were being bred to bands of mares that were daughters and granddaughters of Old Sorrel.

Old Sorrel was included in that first Quarter Horse stud book in 1940. He died in 1945 at age thirty.

Old Sorrel's descendants could do it all. They excelled, and continue to excel, in racing, cutting, and roping, as well as in halter and pleasure classes.

A prime example of Old Sorrel lineage that could win at halter was Wimpy P1, who became an outstanding sire in his own right. Wimpy was sired by one of Old Sorrel's greatest sons, Solis. As a young horse, Wimpy was named Grand Champion halter stallion at the 1941 Southwestern Exposition and Stock Show in Fort Worth, Texas. The fledgling American Quarter Horse Association had decreed that the champion of that show would receive registration number one in the stud book, thus the P1 behind Wimpy's name.

Today, a statue of Wimpy, donated by the Kleberg family, stands in front of the AQHA headquarters in Amarillo, Texas.

Old Sorrel helped establish the famed breeding program of King Ranch.

Two additional horses should be included in the discussion of early-day foundation sires, though their pedigrees cannot be traced with certainty. One was Traveler and the other was Old Fred. We are indebted to Denhardt for researching them.

Traveler's history traces back to Eastland County, Texas, where he first showed up as a workhorse pulling a scraper on the Texas and Pacific Railway. Though a stallion, his quiet temperament apparently permitted him to work in harness beside mares and geldings. Eventually, he was freed from such mundane labor and began his life as a racehorse and later as a breeding stallion. Traveler was between eight and ten years old when he started racing — and winning. When his racing career ended, he stood at stud, his most noteworthy son being Little Joe, foaled in 1904.

Traveler was so successful as a sire that he was the only horse who could approach Peter McCue as

Wimpy was an outstanding grandson of Old Sorrel.

a prolific progenitor in the early years of the AQHA Registry. By January 1, 1948, some 749 of the 11,510 Quarter Horses registered were descendants of Traveler.

Little Joe is significant because he sired, among others, Zantanon, foaled in 1917. Erasmo Flores, a horse breeder in Mexico, purchased Zantanon as a young horse. He was a very successful racehorse in Mexico, but, reportedly, was not well cared for. Texas breeder Manuel Benevides Volpe, who had long admired the horse, bought Zantanon. He told *The Ranchman* in a 1947 article:

"When I bought him in Mexico at fourteen years of age, he was so weak and poor and full of ticks that he could hardly walk."

Volpe nursed Zantanon back to health and stood him at stud. He sired many top quality horses, but the greatest of all was King P234. King sired the famed Poco Bueno, a significant foundation sire for the Quarter Horse breed and whose descendants became top cutting, roping, and all-around ranch horses. Poco Bueno also helped provide the breed with a distinctive look. He stood 14.1 hands tall and in his prime weighed 1,150 pounds. A heavily muscled horse, he spawned what came to be known as the "bulldog" look. For some years that was the "in" look for Quarter Horses.

Like Traveler, Old Fred had a rather humble beginning. He was a golden palomino foaled in about 1893. Though a stallion, he also worked in harness alongside mares and geldings. Denhardt tells the story of Coke Roberds, a prominent Colorado rancher and horse breeder, riding to town with his wife and meeting a freight wagon. The wheel horse hitched to that wagon was Old Fred. Roberds, says Denhardt, was so impressed with the horse he stopped the freighter and bought Old Fred on the spot.

Old Fred became a successful racehorse and then a successful sire, and not just in the Quarter Horse breed. Both he and Traveler show up in some Paint and Appaloosa pedigrees.

The growing Quarter Horse industry also incorporated Kleberg's specific use of the Thoroughbred in breeding programs. Perhaps the most influential Thoroughbred was Three Bars, a horse who would be in the vortex of an AQHA controversy over admitting Thoroughbred blood. Foaled in April 1940 near Lexington, Kentucky, Three Bars overcame a handicap to be a successful racehorse. Despite having severe circulatory problems in a hind leg, Three Bars won a number of races during a four-year career. When he was six, he set a track record over five furlongs at the Phoenix, Arizona, fairgrounds, going the distance in :57⅗. Three Bars also was blazing fast over 440 yards, but didn't have the stamina for distance races of a mile or more.

Three Bars was by a stallion named Percentage, and his dam was Myrtle Dee. She set a speed record for five and a half furlongs at an Ohio track. Myrtle Dee's dam was Civil Maid, a granddaughter of Ben Brush, who won the Kentucky Derby in 1896.

At the age of sixteen, Myrtle Dee, while in foal to Percentage, was purchased at a sale as part of a package of several mares. The buyers, Kentuckians Jack Goode, Ned Brent, and Bill Talbot, had formed a partnership. The mare was turned out on Brent's farm in Bourbon County, Kentucky, where she gave birth to a handsome chestnut colt. The owners thought they had hit the jackpot, so they named the colt Three Bars after the three bars in slot machines.

The colt was indeed very fast in sprint races, but then the circulatory problem surfaced. Some days he would be fine, and on others he was unable to run. The three partners sold the horse to Beckham Stivers for three hundred dollars. Three

Bars went through several owners, eventually winding up in Arizona, where in 1945 he was spotted by a cowboy named Sid Vail. Sid and his wife, Mayola, had a small ranch near Douglas, Arizona, and they were always on the lookout for fast horses.

The horse now carried a price tag of $10,000, which Vail paid. By the next year, Three Bars had recovered from his leg problem and returned to the track. He did very well and was retired in 1947. He stood at Vail's ranch through 1951, but didn't breed very many mares.

Walter Merrick of Sayre, Oklahoma, the era's most prominent breeder of quarter-mile running horses, knew the stallion was just what he needed. He leased Three Bars for two years and took the horse to Oklahoma in 1952.

It was a turbulent time in the Quarter Horse Registry with a huge controversy centered on the question of whether additional Thoroughbred blood ought to be permitted in the breed. Ultimately, the proponents of adding Thoroughbred blood prevailed.

Merrick, who thought infusions of Thoroughbred blood would be good for the Quarter Horse, ignored the controversy and bred Three Bars to his own

Three Bars infused Thoroughbred blood into the modern Quarter Horse.

mares, including ones sired by the likes of Joe Hancock and Midnight Jr. Merrick also bred outside mares, filling Three Bars' book with seventy mares at a three hundred dollar stud fee.

After one year at Merrick's, Vail decided he wanted Three Bars back in Arizona. However, he did offer to sell Three Bars to Merrick, pricing the stallion at $50,000. Vail thought the price was fair, based on the fact that early offspring of Three Bars, such as Bardella, were winning sprint races. Bardella, rated AAAT (a very high speed-index rating), became champion Quarter-running two-year-old and champion Quarter running three-year-old in 1952 and 1953, respectively.

Merrick couldn't afford the $50,000 price tag, and, instead, year after year, hauled his mares to the stallion, first in Arizona and after 1955 to California, where the Vails had moved. California was a hotbed of Quarter Horse racing, and Three Bars was growing in popularity as a stallion. The word was out that if you wanted to win, you had better breed to Three Bars or one of his sons. Eventually, Three Bars' stud fee reached $10,000.

In 1967, when Three Bars was twenty-seven, Vail surprised Merrick by offering to let him have the stallion so that he could take him back to Oklahoma for the rest of his life. Merrick quickly accepted. Three Bars was still siring foals. He died in 1968 at the Merrick ranch.

Three Bars passed on not only his great speed but also his excellent conformation and great disposition.

AQHA records show that he sired 558 offspring, and many were champions in all facets of competition. Four were named AQHA Supreme Champions in the show ring; twenty-nine were AQHA Champions; fourteen were racing champions; and sixty-four were racing stakes winners.

There have been a great many influential sires involved in the development of the Quarter Horse.

The ones discussed above were picked because they demonstrate that through the years a thread often connects great horses of the past to those of the present. In this case the thread connects sires such as the Godolphin Arabian, the Darley Arabian, Janus, Sir Archy, Steel Dust, Shiloh, Dan Tucker, Peter McCue, Hickory Bill, and Old Sorrel. There were a great many random and chance matings along the way, but in many cases, especially in the later years, horsemen had a vision of what the ideal Quarter Horse should be and structured breeding programs to realize that goal. Eventually, breeders of these horses, headed by Denhardt, decided that a stud book should be established, and the AQHA came into being.

Now, a real effort was being made to record breedings and births and to track pedigrees. This was something new to the emerging breed. In the early days, whether in the East or Southwest, no particular effort was made to establish sprint horses as a breed. The good horses that demonstrated speed and an ability to work cattle were crossed with existing stock that might include Arabian, Morgan, Standardbred, or draft bloodlines.

Adding to the difficulty in tracing pedigrees in those early years was the custom of naming horses after their owners. Sometimes when ownership changed, so did the name of the horse. That approach changed with the creation of the AQHA and what developed into sophisticated record keeping.

Not only is the Quarter Horse enjoying unparalleled popularity in the United States today, but the breed has also become highly popular in Europe and on other continents, such as Australia.

All the different influences on the western horse created a great deal of diversity. The western horse came in different sizes and with different skills. It also came in a great variety of colors and patterns. This diversity would lead to development of breeds of horses based on color and patterns of color.

Western Horses of Color

8

The versatile Appaloosa has gone from being highly prized to hunted over its long history.

Colorful horses have long fascinated man. In the caves of central Europe, archeologists have discovered ancient drawings of Appaloosas or Paints, some of which date to about 20,000 B.C., long before horses were domesticated.

How horses developed this elaborate coloration is a genetic mystery. One theory is that these horses evolved in an area with distinct patterns of light and shadow, and that the horses' spots and divergent color patterns emerged through the generations as protection from predators, just as was the case with giraffes and zebras. Whatever the source of their color, Appaloosas and Paints have become an integral part of the western horse.

The Appaloosa

The history of the Appaloosa, and the corresponding depiction in artwork, is as fascinating and colorful as the horse itself. For example, a scabbard discovered in Austria dating back to 1,000 B.C. was decorated with horses bearing typical Appaloosa coloration. Chinese artwork that dates back to at least 500 B.C., including vases and wall hangings, depicts horses with colorful spotted patterns.

These horses were highly valued and sought after in the civilized world. Eventually, the Appaloosa found its way to Europe, and by the mid-seventeenth century, Appaloosas were much favored in the French court of King Louis XIV as both saddle mounts and coach horses.

The first horse of Appaloosa coloring to be imported to England arrived in 1685. Not much is known about that horse or where it originated other than its name — Bloody Buttocks — which may have arisen from an archaic belief that the horse's spots resulted from its having sweated blood.

The first Appaloosas to set hoof in North America arrived with the Spaniards. Two of the horses brought by Cortez are believed to have had

Appaloosa or Paint coloration. As more Appaloosas arrived in Mexico, known then as New Spain, many landed in the hands of Native Americans in the wake of the Pueblo uprising in the 1600s.

As tribes traded or rustled horses from each other, the Appaloosa found its way into the dry climate of the Palouse River country of eastern Washington, northeastern Oregon, and the Idaho panhandle. The mighty Snake and Columbia rivers also course through this region. The area proved to be an excellent breeding ground for Appaloosas. The southeast corner of Palouse country was home to the Nez Perce Indians, who are credited with breeding quality Appaloosa horses that were the envy of other tribes and even the white men.

Meriwether Lewis, the famous explorer of the Northwest, recorded in his journal that the Nez Perce had horses similar in quality to the highly bred equines in his native Virginia. Proof that the Nez Perce were selective breeders includes the way in which they dealt with inferior stallions. While most tribes, following the custom of the Spaniards who had brought horses to the new land, left their stallions intact, the Nez Perce gelded those deemed unworthy of serving as herd sires.

The Lewis and Clark expedition saw many horses with Appaloosa coloring. One might assume the Nez Perce preferred colorful horses, but quality counted most. Having a swift and sure-footed horse meant more to a Nez Perce warrior than having a colorful one. The Nez Perce horses, according to descriptions by Lewis, were strong, sturdy, and larger than the wild horses roaming across the plains.

White men traveling through the Palouse River country gave the name Appaloosa to the breed. In the beginning, they called these well-bred animals "a Palouse horse." Later the term would be "A Palousy" or "Appaloosie." The names, it seems, were used to distinguish these quality horses from the more common-appearing Mustangs, Pintos, Paints, and solid-colored horses used by other Native American tribes.

Other tribes and white men passing through the area often sought out the Nez Perce for their selectively bred horses. Frequently, however, the Nez Perce used these opportunities to further their breeding program by selling or trading geldings or stallions considered inferior.

By the late 1800s the Nez Perce owned thousands of Appaloosas. Unfortunately, the winds of change carried seeds of disaster for this proud, advanced tribe of horse breeders. White settlers eyed their land and decided that they, not the Nez Perce, should be farming and ranching on it.

The inevitable conflict broke out in 1877. The U.S. government ordered the Nez Perce to a reservation in Idaho. They refused, claiming they had ancestral rights to the land on which they lived in the Wallowa Valley. Soldiers were sent out, and the Nez Perce, the same tribe that had welcomed the starving Lewis and Clark expedition into its midst seventy-two years earlier, fought back.

The Nez Perce quickly realized that, despite some battlefield successes, they were outnumbered and could not win against the white man's army. They decided they would flee to Montana and if the white men pursued, the tribe would continue into Canada and join forces with Sitting Bull, who had fled there after the Little Big Horn battle against George A. Custer and the Seventh Cavalry.

Before the ordeal ended, the Nez Perce covered more than 1,300 miles, over precipitous mountain trails and across swollen rivers. The army came in pursuit but wasn't able to force the tribe's surrender until the Nez Perce paused for rest, mistakenly believing they had crossed the border into Canada.

That the pursuing army could not defeat the Nez Perce, and, in fact, lost some running engagements is noteworthy, but that the tribe was traveling with women and children and carrying all of its possessions makes its flight nothing short of incredible.

Much credit for this epic feat goes to the Appaloosas, which were superior to the army mounts.

Both sides incurred losses. When the trek began, the Nez Perce warriors were nearly three hundred strong. When Chief Joseph finally surrendered in October 1877, only eighty-seven remained, forty of whom were wounded.

The Nez Perce horses that survived the fighting did not outlive the aftermath. Fearing that the Nez Perce would still pose a formidable fighting force with their Appaloosas, the army ordered that every Appaloosa found should be killed.

In one historical account, four hundred Appaloosas were driven into a ravine while soldiers on the high banks methodically shot them down.

The missionaries supported the army's quest, believing the Nez Perce would first have to be deprived of their horses to become peaceful farmers who accepted Christianity. Then, both the army and the missionaries realized that without horses, the Nez Perce would be unable to farm. Faced with this dilemma, the army came up with what it considered a compromise. The Indians could keep the few remaining horses, but they had to be crossed with draft horses. Appaloosas not crossed with draft horses, the army decreed, would be shot.

The army successfully nullified the Nez Perce as a fighting force. Deprived of their Appaloosa horses, they wound up on reservations and never again went on the warpath.

It wasn't until the Appaloosa was nearly extinct that action was taken to save the breed and begin its rebirth. The effort was led by Claude Thompson of Moro, Oregon, who in 1938 helped form the Appaloosa Horse Club, officially adopting the name for the breed. It has remained the registry for these colorful horses.

When Thompson and his supporters launched their effort, many horses of color sported draft horse blood as a result of the army's earlier edict and few Appaloosas of the original strain remained.

To return the breed to the type bred by the Nez Perce, Thompson reasoned, original bloodlines of horses brought here by the Spaniards were needed. To that effect, he began breeding some of his draft-Appaloosa mares to Ferras, an Arabian stallion.

Foaled in 1932, the chestnut Ferras was sired by *Ferdin and out of *Rasima, two Arabians imported from the Crabbet Stud of England, famous for producing quality Arabian horses. In 1945 Thompson bred Ferras to an Appaloosa mare named Painter's Marvel, herself a granddaughter of Ferras. The following year she produced a colt that became a show champion and a sire of champions.

The colt, bay and white with bay spots, was named Red Eagle. As he matured, he competed in the Appaloosa horse shows being held to bring attention to the breed. In 1951 Red Eagle was named National Champion Appaloosa stallion. (The first-ever National Championship Appaloosa Show was held in Lewistown, Idaho, in 1948.)

After that victory, actor John Derek purchased Red Eagle, planning to feature him in a film. The film was never made, and Derek sold Red Eagle to Thomas Clay of the 1001 Ranch in Caliente, Nevada. At the 1001 Ranch, Red Eagle sired eighty-one foals that earned several national championships and went on to be noteworthy breeding animals.

Appaloosa Horse Club members recognized, as demonstrated by Thompson, that they had to cross the Appaloosas of the day with other breeds to successfully re-establish the Appaloosa as a breed. They also allowed registration of horses that demonstrated Appaloosa characteristics but that had unverified or unidentified parentage.

Those characteristics included a variety of color coat patterns, such as blanket over the hips or leopard, which featured spots all over the body, white sclera of the eye, striped hooves, and parti-colored or mottled skin about the nostrils, lips, and reproductive organs.

A number of horses registered as Appaloosas through the years were solid-colored. The Appaloosa Horse Club, for some years, permitted these horses to compete in classes alongside Appaloosas of color. That has changed, at least to a degree. Solid-colored foals born on or after January 1, 2002, must be the result of two Appaloosa-registered parents to be eligible for the CPO (certified pedigree option) program. Solid-colored foals resulting from outcrosses to Quarter Horses, Thoroughbreds, and Arabians are no longer eligible.

Through the years the genetic makeup of certain Appaloosas has been controversial. A case in point is a stallion named Wapiti, foaled in 1955. Wapiti had all of the Appaloosa characteristics when he was born, but his sire was a solid-colored registered Quarter Horse and so was his dam.

Some thought Wapiti was a genetic freak. However, research into his pedigree and the recollection of old-time horsemen who were breeding horses of color before Thompson and his friends founded the Appaloosa Horse Club revealed different information. Wapiti demonstrated that Quarter Horses and Appaloosas shared some foundation pedigrees.

When the American Quarter Horse Association formed in the early 1940s, it followed the Appaloosa Horse Club in accepting into its stud book a number of horses that traced to the famed Coke Roberds' breeding program. Roberds ran a ranch in western Colorado, after settling in Texas and then Oklahoma.

In the late 1800s Roberds ventured into the breeding business. He orchestrated a breeding between a stallion called The Circus Horse, because it had been purchased from a circus that wintered nearby, and a mare of racing blood that Roberds owned. The result was a colorful stallion with a spotted coat that Roberds, interestingly, named Arab. The horse was loudly colored, and Roberds often hitched him to the buggy for trips to town.

Later, Roberds bought nine Steel Dust mares and bred at least some of them to the colorful Arab. Roberds also purchased a Thoroughbred stallion named Primero. The horse was a stocking-legged, blazed-faced chestnut. He bred Primero to his mares, some of which carried the blood of the colorful Arab. Some of the foals had Appaloosa color and characteristics. In 1908 Roberds shipped Primero and some mares by train from Oklahoma to his new ranch in Colorado. The train wrecked en route and Primero was killed. One survivor was a Primero daughter, a roan Appaloosa.

She later was bred to Bob H, a son of AQHA foundation sire Old Fred, and produced an Appaloosa filly called the Blue Roan Mare. When the two registries opened their books, horses of these lines, including the Blue Roan Mare, were accepted by both organizations, thus paving the way for two solid-colored registered Quarter Horses to produce a colorful Appaloosa when two recessive genes linked up, as was the case with Wapiti.

Wapiti started his career as a riding horse and pack horse but later was put to stud and began siring National Champions in both halter and performance.

Wapiti's lineage could be traced because breeders along the way kept track of matings and births. Unfortunately, many of the horses bred and raised in those early years appear in Appaloosa pedigrees as "unknown" or "unregistered" because a number of breeders did not keep accurate records, if they kept records at all. In other cases, a horse with Appaloosa coloring and characteristics might show up with no one having a clue about its parentage.

Joker B. is another Appaloosa whose lineage traces to the Coke Roberds breeding era. Foaled in 1941, Joker B. was sired by a registered Quarter Horse and was out of an unregistered blue roan mare named Blue Vitriol, who was a product of Coke Roberds' aforementioned breeding program. Jack Casement, who owned Joker B.'s sire and dam, was shocked when the foal was born with a huge white blanket full of black spots.

Casement gave the little misfit to his wife, and she sold him to a neighbor for $250 because she wanted money for a vacuum cleaner. Joker B. changed hands a number of times and along the way became a bulldogging, hazing, and pick-up horse on the rodeo circuit.

Joker B.'s sixth owner was Bill Benoist, who decided the stallion should be used in his breeding program. Joker B. immediately began siring offspring that became champions in the show ring.

By now his value had increased well beyond the purchase price of a vacuum cleaner. In 1959, when Joker B. was eighteen, Carl Miles, a highly successful Texas oilman, purchased him for $10,000. Miles promoted Joker B. through hundreds of magazine ads and a wide variety of other approaches. The stallion and Miles' Cee Bar Ranch were even featured on NBC's *Today Show*.

Miles did not stint in the mare category and owned some of the breed's best, which he bred to Joker B. The result was one champion Appaloosa after another. These champions went on to produce champions of their own, generating Joker B.'s eventual elevation into the Appaloosa Hall of Fame.

A short time before Joker B.'s death, Miles began looking for a replacement for the aging stallion, now owned by a syndicate of four. He found Prince Plaudit.

Prince Plaudit traced back to Old Fred, and Miles was convinced he would be a stallion around which to build a breeding program. He was right. With Miles conducting an all-out promotional campaign, Prince Plaudit first established himself as a champion show horse and then as a sire of multiple champions. Prince Plaudit was sold at auction in 1974 for $260,000 and shortly thereafter was syndicated for $300,000, at a rate of $50,000 per share.

Finally, the Appaloosa was being returned to its status as an excellent western horse. Its new owners were breeding selectively just as their Nez Perce predecessors had done.

Paint Horses

Rebecca Lockhart of Ryan, Oklahoma, is credited with founding the American Paint Horse Association (APHA). In November 2000, she was inducted into the National Cowgirl Museum and Hall of Fame in Fort Worth, Texas, a testament to her accomplishments.

The Paint registry's goal is to produce a horse with a distinctive color pattern and stock horse body type. To be eligible for registration, a Paint horse must come from stock registered with the APHA, the American Quarter Horse Association, or The Jockey Club (Thoroughbreds).

Some people have confused Paints and Pintos, but there is a distinct difference. The Paint must qualify for registration by carrying the bloodline or bloodlines listed above, while the Pinto Horse Association is a color registry. This means horses of any type or breeding are eligible for the Pinto registry as long as they have the spotted coloration.

For registration and breeding purposes, American Paint Horses are categorized by their specific color patterns. Those patterns, as explained by the APHA, are as follows:

Tobiano (tow be yah' no): This pattern is distinguished by head markings like those of solid-colored horses — plain or with a blaze, strip, star, or snip. All four of the tobiano's legs are usually white, at least below the knees and hocks. The spots are regular and distinctly oval or round and extend down the neck and chest, giving the appearance of a shield. A tobiano can have the dark color on one or both flanks, although the overall coat may be either predominantly dark or white. The tail is often two colors. (Tobiano and overo are Spanish words that describe in brief the two color patterns. The registry expanded upon them to provide detailed descriptions of the color patterns.)

Overo (oh vair' oh): This pattern may also be either predominantly dark or white. However, the white on an overo typically does not cross the back of the horse between its withers and tail. Generally, one or all four legs are dark. The overo tends to have bold white head markings, such as a bald face, and irregular, scattered markings on the body. The horse's tail is usually one color.

Tovero (tow vair' oh): Because not all coat patterns fit neatly into either the tobiano or overo category, the APHA expanded its classifications to include tovero, which describes horses that have characteristics of both the tobiano and overo patterns.

In the 1800s and on into the 1900s, these horses of color were referred to by various names, such as pinto, paint, skewbald, and piebald.

The first move to establish a registry for spotted horses came in the late 1950s when a group banded together and organized the Pinto Horse Association.

However, they were dedicated to preserving the color patterns rather than establishing a particular breed. Thus a Pinto can be an Arabian, a Saddlebred, a Quarter Horse, a combination of all of the above, or a variety of others, just as long as it is spotted.

Considering the popularity of Paint horses today, it is difficult to imagine that in the 1940s, '50s, and even early '60s, they were considered inferior.

For some reason, horsemen of that era thought that spots equated with a lack of ability and quality. In the early 1960s Rebecca Lockhart spoke up in favor of establishing a registry for stock-type Paint horses with definite bloodlines instead of just color. The Paint envisioned by this group was to be a stock horse first, with color to go with it.

"Sometime in 1960," Lockhart was quoted in an article published by *The Appaloosa News* in 2001, "I started calling on my friends. I wanted to know if there was anyone besides me interested in starting a registry for these horses. When someone would say they were interested, I would write down the information and put the slip of paper in a box on my kitchen table. Before long, my table was covered with slips of paper."

Much of the stock horse establishment of that day opposed the idea of a Paint horse registry, but that didn't deter Lockhart.

Supported by three prominent horsemen from the Gainesville, Texas, area — E.J. Hudspeth, Truman Moody, and Charlie Moore — Lockhart decided to stage a horse show. She and her small group of supporters contacted all of the Paint horse owners they knew in Oklahoma and Texas and asked them to bring their Paints to Waurika, Oklahoma. It was a small show, but a successful one, that set the stage for bigger and better things.

Next, the group boldly approached the directors of the Southwestern Exposition and Fat Stock Show in Fort Worth and asked them to include a class for Paints. After much discussion, the directors approved an open color class for the 1961 show.

Lockhart and her friends decided the time had

Once considered inferior because of their distinctive coats, Paints now enjoy great popularity with horse owners.

come to form a registry. Lockhart called a meeting for February 16, 1962, at the Curtwood Motel in Gainesville. A grand total of seventeen people attended. Despite being few in number, the group forged ahead, writing and adopting a constitution and bylaws. Officers and directors were elected, and the group gave itself the name American Paint Stock Horse Association.

Lockhart was named secretary and for a time became "Miss Everything" to the fledgling organization. Sitting at her kitchen table in August 1962, she recorded the pedigree of the first Paint Horse in the new registry. It was a black-and-white tobiano stallion named Bandits Pinto, owned by the Flying M Ranch of McKinney, Texas.

By year's end, Lockhart had attracted 150 members and had registered 250 horses. The next year, she turned her responsibilities over to Ralph Morrison, who became the group's first executive secretary. The headquarters moved to Amarillo, Texas, and that year the group chartered its first regional club — the Gulf Coast Paint Horse Club. The group held its first show the same year, giving away a saddle and nineteen high-point trophies.

In 1964 the headquarters moved to Fort Worth, where it remains today, though now the offices are in a modern $5.8 million building. By the end of 1964, the association had registered 1,269 horses, had 1,005 members, six regional clubs, and had hosted its first national show with 134 entries from twelve states.

Meanwhile, in Abilene, Texas, another group of spotted-horse lovers had organized the American Paint Quarter Horse Association. The group could never gain momentum, and in 1965, after lengthy debate, the two associations merged and became the American Paint Horse Association with 1,300 members and 3,800 horses registered.

In recent years interest in these colorful horses soared, turning the APHA into the fastest-growing registry in the equine world. The year 2000 witnessed two milestones for the association: The number of horses registered surpassed the 500,000 mark and membership topped 100,000.

The association continues to grow. Both of the above numbers were quickly eclipsed in 2001, with the number of registered horses approaching 600,000 and membership increasing steadily and rapidly.

Some of the same foundation sires that are the cornerstones of the Quarter Horse breed also show up in Paint pedigrees. A number of these sires possess a recessive color gene that is expressed in "cropouts" — offspring of two solid-colored horses that are born with color.

Quarter Horse foundation lines in which cropouts have occurred most frequently include those of Joe Reed, through his descendant Leo; Little Joe, by the legendary Traveler; Peter McCue, owned as an older horse by Roberds; and Skipper W and Nick Shoemaker, the latter two being linebred Old Fred horses.

While horses of color — both Appaloosas and Paints — have much in common with their solid-colored brethren in the AQHA, all three breeds are now advancing along their own paths and have been instrumental in molding the modern-day western horse.

Palomino and Buckskin

Both the Palomino and Buckskin are color registries, meaning that horses of various breeds can be registered as Palomino or Buckskin as long as they have the required coat color. Both of them deserve mention because some quality Palominos and Buckskins have the western horse look and breeding and helped to promulgate it. For example the great Quarter Horse and Appaloosa progenitor Old Fred was golden palomino.

The Palomino Horse Breeders of America (PHBA) originated in California in the 1930s and is now located in Tulsa, Oklahoma. To be registered, horses must stand between fourteen to seventeen hands high and exhibit the body color — with variations ranging from light to dark — of a U.S. fourteen-karat gold coin. The mane and tail must be white with not more than fifteen percent dark, sorrel, or chestnut hairs. There are three basic registry divisions: stock type, which are primarily Quarter Horses; Golden American Saddlebred; and the pleasure type, represented by the likes of Morgans, Arabians, and Tennessee Walking Horses. The PHBA says there are about 71,000 registered Palomino horses.

There are two registries for Buckskin horses. The oldest is the American Buckskin Registry Association, established in 1963. The other registry is the International Buckskin Horse Registry, which was incorporated in 1971.

The American Buckskin Registry maintains that many modern buckskin, dun, red dun, and grulla hues trace to the mustang and the Spanish Barb. Other buckskins brought to the country, according to the registry, can be traced to the Norwegian Dun, a descendant of the nearly extinct Tarpan horses. Horses with buckskin color can be found in all breed types.

The International Buckskin Horse Registry lists 22,700 horses. The American Buckskin Registry, which also registers buckskin ponies and mules lists approximately 20,000 horses, 3,000 ponies, and 1,500 mules.

It's no wonder the western horses of color have become so popular. Like their close kin, the Quarter Horse, these colorful animals are versatile and kind, making them perfect mounts for the many tasks their human counterparts ask of them.

A Palomino in competition.

A Buckskin at work.

The Western Horse
Goes to War

9

From domestication until after World War II, the horse was used to wage war, doing everything from pulling heavy artillery to carrying cavalrymen into the fight. A horse made a soldier more effective. Not only did a mounted soldier have a physical advantage over a foot soldier because of mobility and the power of the horse, he also had a psychological advantage. The thundering charge of cavalry could strike fear in a soldier who had only two legs and, perhaps, a sword or lance on which to rely.

Cortez' invasion of Mexico clearly demonstrated the value of mounted fighters. With only a handful of soldiers, Cortez defeated a force of thousands. The Aztecs were in abject fear of the mounted soldiers because they thought the horsemen were gods, with man and horse being one.

Many of the horses employed in war formed the genetic pool that produced today's western horse. We can only speculate about which great bloodlines were lost on the battlefield. Only the strongest, toughest, and most able horses survived the conflicts, and the bloodlines that emerged from these crucibles resulted in horses with strong bones and muscles, an inner toughness, and, often, excellent dispositions. War horses, after all, were expected to be calm and manageable, even when shells were bursting around them.

Some of war's effects on the western horse are more subtle. The Native Americans, for example, became experts at stealth, surprise, and camouflage when waging wars on other tribes or white men.

Some tribes discovered that using horses of varying colors at different times of the year aided their camouflage efforts. Subsequently, Native Americans probably bred for certain colors. Duns, roans, and light sorrels, for example, blended in with the prairie colors in summer and fall, while white horses and palominos matched the color of the landscape in late fall and winter. Gray and roan colors blended in with sagebrush. The Paint horse with its dark and white splotches could be changed from light to dark, by rubbing clay into one color or the other.

The Revolutionary War also shaped today's western horse. The colonists who rose up against the British were carried to battle on their tough and fast Chickasaw horses. Once there, the riders often dismounted and fought on foot, firing from the cover of trees and rocks as they had learned from the Native Americans. Neither the British nor the colonists used cavalry charges as a customary strategy.

The colonists often put their steeds to better use than the British did. The British forces consisted primarily of trained infantry, so most of their horses pulled cannons, packed tents and other supplies, and provided mounts for loyalist guides and British officers. With few good roads to travel, the British often found themselves inching along with their ponderous army. The rebel militia, on the other hand, traveling lightly and mounted on their Chickasaws or Chickasaw crossbreds, would join forces for a battle and then rapidly disappear into the woods and hills.

The American forces pretty much comprised lightly organized militia, except, perhaps, for the Continental Army under George Washington's command. Militia members pretty much came and went as they pleased. When it was time for planting, they might leave the army to attend to their fields, with their plows often being pulled by the same horses that carried them into battle. The fall harvest could prompt a similar exodus. However, whenever word spread that the British were on the move in a particular area, militia members would mount their horses and report for duty.

The Chickasaw or Chickasaw crossbred horses owned by many of the colonists were solidly built, tough, hardy animals that could quickly negotiate the forests and hill country, subsisting on forage.

When word spread across the mountain regions of the Carolinas and Virginia, including the areas that would become Tennessee and Kentucky, that Charles Cornwallis and his British forces were preparing a full-scale invasion of North Carolina, rebel volunteers were ready.

The British had swept northward through Georgia and South Carolina in 1778 and 1779. Believing South Carolina was pretty much in the crown's proverbial pocket, Cornwallis took aim at North Carolina in 1780.

Cornwallis had the largest force of the three parallel British units moving northward in September 1780. Colonel Banastre "Bloody" Tarleton commanded the light infantry and cavalry, and Major Patrick Ferguson headed the Tory command. It was Ferguson's duty to protect the western flank of Cornwallis' army. Ferguson had a total force of about eleven hundred men.

By September 25, 1780, one thousand rebel volunteers had gathered at Sycamore Shoals on the banks of the Watauga River, near the present site of Elizabethton, Tennessee. Most of them were mounted on their own horses and carrying their own provisions. They all had one thing in common: a strong desire to defeat Major Ferguson and the Tories fighting under him.

On September 26 the militia headed east and south into the mountains, traveling through boot-high snow. The riders covered ninety mountain miles in five days and then were joined by another force of 350 men from two counties in North Carolina.

Ferguson, meanwhile, had taken up a defensive position atop Kings Mountain, about fifty miles west of Charlotte, then part of South Carolina, where Cornwallis' main army was encamped. Ferguson had advanced into North Carolina but decided to fall back to be closer to Cornwallis at Charlotte.

Ferguson felt his position on Kings Mountain was impregnable. On the surface his assumption appeared correct. In the rolling red-clay country known as the Piedmont, which lies between the mountains and the coastal plain, the peak of Kings Mountain suddenly rises, gradually extending southward, containing escarpments and abutments on either side. Ferguson positioned his men on one of the southernmost spurs, a stony summit six hundred yards long.

When the rebel force learned that Ferguson appeared to be heading back toward Charlotte, a council of war selected nine hundred horsemen who would ride hard and intercept him.

The men rode through a rainstorm all that night and the following morning, but they were unable to intercept Ferguson before he had established his defensive position on Kings Mountain. Discovering that Ferguson was already entrenched, the rebels attacked anyway. Fighting on foot — though some also fought from horseback — the rebels carried the day. A measure of credit must go to their mounts because the rebels wouldn't have reached the battle site in a timely manner without the tough, resilient ancestors of today's western horse.

One of the few battles that involved a cavalry charge on the part of the rebel army occurred

January 17, 1781, the last year of the war, at a place called Hannah's Cowpens in South Carolina.

"Bloody" Tarleton, known primarily among the rebels for his brutality, horse thefts, and looting, was in command of British cavalry and light infantry whose goal it was to defeat the rebels in South Carolina. The rebels were commanded by Daniel Morgan, with the cavalry under the command of William Washington, a relative of Commander-In-Chief George Washington.

When the British advanced on the rebel position in a location where cattle had been gathered and penned, thus the name Cowpens, Morgan had his expert marksmen hide in tall grass on a hillside while a small contingent served as decoys at the bottom of the incline. When Tarleton, his cavalry, and infantry advanced, the decoys fired off a round and then retreated. The British, thinking they had routed their foes, charged after them. When they came within range of Morgan's riflemen the charging British were mowed down. As their line wavered, Washington and the cavalry charged down the hill into the midst of the British horsemen. After a brief fight the British cavalry dropped their sabers and surrendered. Tarleton, however, managed to escape.

On October 19, 1781, Cornwallis surrendered to General George Washington in Yorktown, Virginia, ending the war. Washington was an excellent horseman and throughout the conflict was mounted on a sorrel horse named Nelson. Washington had named the horse after his friend Thomas Nelson, the governor of Virginia. A prominent horse breeder, Washington had imported Nelson's Arabian sire. When the war ended, Nelson was retired to Washington's Mount Vernon farm and was never ridden again.

In ensuing decades, the horse population burgeoned in the growing United States so that by the time of the Civil War hundreds of thousands of horses were pressed into service.

Horses and mules usually served about seven and a half months; the average cavalry horse only lasted six months before being lost to death, illness, or over-work. Kentucky, alone, which has always been a horse-breeding center, lost approximately 90,000 horses and 37,000 mules during the Civil War.

Overall, depending on which estimate one wants to accept, somewhere between one and a half million and three million horses and mules lost their lives in the Civil War. Most of these horses labored under a cloak of anonymity, with names and pedigrees lost to history.

Some of the "work horses" of that era — the ones that would pull the cannons and wagons for both sides — were crosses between the eastern horse and Spanish stock that had moved eastward from the Southwest a century earlier. Though they were strong, tough, and hardy, the Spanish horses were considered too small for farm work and pulling large wagons in the cities. As a result, many mares carrying Spanish blood were mated with draft-type stallions. A number of these mares also were bred to mammoth jacks to produce strong and durable mules.

In the beginning of the Civil War, southern forces had far better mounts than their northern counterparts. The South, with its plantations and somewhat cavalier lifestyle, bred horses of high quality, both for racing and as spirited and fancy mounts for the plantation owners and their families.

(Many of these horses carried the bloodlines of horses that today would be called American Saddlebreds. In those days they were called Denmarks because one of the main progenitors was a horse named Gaines' Denmark. While the Denmarks or Saddlebreds aren't considered western horses, some of their blood would find its way into the veins of horses that eventually would be known as western horses.)

When war broke out, many of the southern volunteers opted for the cavalry. They had to provide their own horses, but they were paid an additional forty cents a day to do so. If the horse was killed or disabled in battle, the southern cavalryman was paid the appraised value of the animal and provided with a thirty-day furlough to return home and find a replacement. This particular provision would come to haunt the southern army because often when the fighting was heaviest, the number of furloughed cavalrymen seeking new mounts on the home front would be the highest.

Nevertheless, the South had a cavalry of elite horses, ridden by excellent horsemen used to living outdoors. They were a force to be reckoned with, at least during the first years of the war.

By contrast, the Union army concentrated much more heavily on infantry and artillery. The Union's cavalry seemed constantly to lack horses, even though the North had more horses. The South had about 2,877,000 horses and mules, while the North had about 4,523,000, according to the 1860 U.S. census.

In the early months of the war, the Union army had only six cavalry regiments. As the war continued, the North realized the importance of a strong cavalry and by 1863 the bluecoats had thirty-six cavalry regiments.

In the South, horses were getting harder to come by. After Vicksburg fell on July 4, 1863, western-type horses from Texas, Arkansas, and Missouri could no longer be funneled to the Confederate army. Matters worsened when the northern armies occupied Missouri, Kentucky, and northern Mississippi, giving the Union reign over the horses in those states.

Life for a horse in the Civil War, no matter what his type or breeding, was grim. Many were killed in battle, but a great many also died from disease and injury and some literally were ridden to death. When a horse faltered in the line of march, it was left behind, but only for a short time. It was the job of the rearguard to shoot all horses that the advancing troops had abandoned. The theory was that if the horse recovered from exhaustion or wounds, it would be available to the enemy.

In the wake of a battle, burial details would dig graves for the fallen soldiers while the dead horses were dragged into piles and burned.

Often the war horses were saddle sore from many hours in service, enduring all kinds of weather with little to eat and only muddy river water to drink. The result of this trial by fire was survival of the fittest — tough horses that contributed to the genetic pool of today's western horse.

Morgans provided a number of mounts for the northern cavalry. Seven Union regiments were mounted on Morgans, including the First Vermont Cavalry, which saw action in seventy-five major battles and skirmishes. Of the regiment's original 1,200 Morgans, fewer than two hundred survived.

The most famous of the Morgans was Rienzi, a horse that carried General Philip Sheridan on a dash made famous by Thomas Buchanan Reed's poem, "Sheridan's Ride." Sheridan rode from Winchester, Virginia, to the Cedar Creek battlefield in the Shenandoah Valley at full gallop, halted a retreat, rallied the troops, and carried the day. Though Reed's poem has the ride covering twenty miles, it was really twelve, but the poem made Sheridan and Rienzi (later renamed Winchester) heroes.

As with Sheridan and Winchester, other Civil War generals and their horses became celebrated teams. The South's Robert E. Lee, for example, rode his white horse, Traveller, in a number of campaigns. Traveller was most likely a Tennessee Walking Horse because of his ambling gait, but there is no indisputable proof of that. The man who sold Traveller to Lee when the horse was four said only that he was of Grey Eagle stock. The horse was fearless in battle, and stories are told of how Lee, just as fearless in the heat of a firefight, sometimes had to be restrained by aides from riding headlong into the conflict, with Traveller eager and willing to carry him into the fray.

Traveller and Lee were not without their troubles. In one instance Lee was on the ground holding

Traveller, when the fractious horse jumped, causing Lee to fall on a stump and break bones in both of his hands. Lee's chief cavalry officer decided Traveller was too much horse for Lee, especially with his injured hands, and procured a small mare for him named Lucy Long. She was a very docile horse and served Lee well until she became pregnant. No details are offered on just how this pregnancy came about, such as what stallion bred her or what kind of foal she had. She was replaced with a tall horse, likely a Thoroughbred, named Ajax, but Lee, a relatively short man, found him too tall and went back to riding Traveller, who remained his mount to the end of the conflict. At the conclusion of the war, Traveller, Lucy Long, and Ajax were retired to Lee's farm in Virginia.

Union General Ulysses S. Grant had three horses. One was an easy-going pacer named Egypt that Grant rode when traveling a long distance over rough ground. Another was a Thoroughbred named Cincinnati, who reportedly was given to him following Grant's victory at Vicksburg. Cincinnati was a son of the great stallion Lexington. Grant was on Cincinnati when he rode up to Appomattox Court House to accept the Confederate surrender in 1865. Grant's third horse was a small animal of obscure background that was captured on the plantation of Joe Davis, brother of Jefferson Davis, president of the Confederacy.

General John Hunt Morgan, the famed Confederate cavalry officer from Kentucky, rode a mare named Black Bess. Her sire came from a famous line of saddle stock that was primarily Canadian Pacer in origin. Her dam was a Thoroughbred. She was a gift to Morgan by a horse breeder at Stonewall Farm near Lexington, Kentucky. Black Bess survived only one year in combat.

Another friend replaced the fallen mare with a Thoroughbred named Glencoe Jr., son of the illustrious sire Glencoe. The gift-giver was a noted Thoroughbred breeder in Kentucky, Alexander K. Richards. At one point, he supplied an entire Confederate cavalry company with mounts and equipment.

Thomas "Stonewall" Jackson rode Little Sorrel, a tough gelding believed to be of Morgan descent. The horse stood less than thirteen hands, yet he carried

During the Civil War, horses played an integral role on both sides.

Jackson indefatigably for miles at a time. Jackson was described as being awkward and ungainly in the saddle, thus making Little Sorrel's feats of endurance even more impressive.

In the early stages of the war, the Confederate cavalry members pretty much had things their own way. Generally better mounted and with better riders, they could ride circles around the Union army, providing valuable information about troop location.

General J.E.B. Stuart, the South's most celebrated cavalry officer, actually did just that. He was colorful, dashing, and flamboyant, and he loved publicity. Lee put up with Stuart's vanity and devil-may-care attitude because the officer and his cavalrymen were dauntless lookouts.

In one celebrated foray, Lee sent Stuart and 1,200 mounted men from Richmond, Virginia, to assess the location and strength of General George B. McClellan's Union forces as they advanced toward the city. Lee had placed his army between McClellan's force and Richmond.

Stuart left Richmond on June 12, 1862, and headed for the Union lines. His unit transcended orders and rode all the way around McClellan's army, traveling some miles through enemy-held territory. Along the way they engaged in running battles and destroyed part of the northern supply line. They returned to the safety of their own lines on July 16.

The Union cavalry later would make its own headlines. During the spring of 1863, General Grant was determined to capture Vicksburg, Mississippi. However, he needed a diversion that would confuse and fragment the Confederate defenders so that he could cross the Mississippi River and position his army.

Grant ordered Colonel Benjamin H. Grierson to take three regiments of his cavalry, numbering about 1,700 men, and ride two hundred miles from Tennessee into Confederate-held territory and cut the railroad line leading into Vicksburg. While Stuart's cavalry were primarily mounted on

"Denmarks," when they rode around Union troops, we can assume that Grierson's cavalry, with ties to the Midwest, were likely mounted on stouter, less fiery steeds that more closely resembled the western horse of today.

When the raid was over, Grierson had exceeded Grant's request. He reported that his cavalrymen had killed and wounded about one hundred of the enemy, captured and paroled more than five hundred prisoners, destroyed between fifty and sixty miles of railroad and telegraph lines, captured and destroyed more than three thousand stands of arms, along with other army stores and property, and captured one thousand horses and mules from the enemy. In the process his command suffered only light casualties.

Making their feat even more impressive was how the men subsisted sixteen days on five days of provisions. Their horses survived on countryside forage.

Obviously, Grierson's cavalrymen were very well mounted for their foray. They traveled more than six hundred miles in sixteen days, their raid coming to an end in Union-held Baton Rouge, Louisiana. Grierson would further report that during the last twenty-eight hours of the march, his mounted troopers covered seventy-six miles, had four engagements with the enemy, and had forded a river that was so swollen, the horses had to swim across it. During those final twenty-eight hours, both men and horses had to go without food and rest.

Once the Civil War ended, the northern cavalryman had another force to subdue — the Plains Native Americans of the West. That effort had been put on the army's back burner during the Civil War.

For this renewed task, the cavalryman's horse turned out to be ill suited. Officers at the time concluded that the cavalryman must be prepared when marching against enemy forces. His horse not only carried its rider, but also was burdened with a saddle, weapon, ammunition, blanket, rations, a feedbag containing oats, halter, hobbles, bed sheet, and other items considered indispensable.

All of this equipment demanded a large horse. The army purchased the offspring of draft (for size) and saddle stock (for durability) crosses that had been bred to Thoroughbreds (for speed).

The Native American, however, didn't bother increasing either the size or the speed of his mount. The smaller, more durable Indian pony could travel for hours. When it tired, the warrior merely switched to another of his horses that would be traveling with the band. The Native American warrior also used only a very light pad-saddle and carried light weapons and perhaps only a robe for warmth. He lived off the land, as did his horse, grazing during brief stops.

By comparison, the larger cavalry horse needed much more food to maintain its weight and strength. Often grass alone was insufficient, and the horse required a supplement of grain.

It is no wonder that the cavalrymen came up short in many a skirmish as the Native American warriors would attack and then escape as the cavalry lumbered along in futile pursuit.

General Sam Houston of Texas reportedly commented in 1859 that American troops couldn't chase Native Americans one day without their (the cavalry's) horses becoming lame. Another problem, he complained, was that the cavalry horses needed grain and that they were campaigning in a country that had no grain.

Frustrated that they couldn't beat their foes in mounted confrontations, the army captured Indian ponies and shot them.

Lieutenant Colonel George A. Custer attacked a Cheyenne Indian village on the Washita River during a snowstorm, killing many warriors and women and children. Custer ordered his men to shoot the 850 ponies captured in the raid.

A cavalry regiment waters its horses.

When Ranald S. MacKenzie, commander of the Fourth U.S. Cavalry defeated the Comanches in Palo Duro Canyon, near present-day Amarillo, Texas, in 1874, MacKenzie ordered the Native American camp burned and had one thousand of the 1,400 captured horses shot. MacKenzie's cavalry officers objected, but to no avail.

Native Americans would get a measure of revenge at the Battle of the Little Big Horn in 1876. The only survivor of that battle, man or beast, from the Seventh Cavalry was a fifteen-hand bay gelding named Comanche, thought to be part Morgan and part mustang — truly a western horse — who was ridden into battle by Captain Myles Keogh. The horse was wounded by at least seven arrows but survived and lived to age twenty-nine.

When the British went to war against two colonies in South Africa in 1899, they took a number of western horses with them, providing a much-needed shot in the arm for American ranchers. The rangelands were in an economic slump with saddle horses being worth next to nothing and cattle prices also low. Horses were selling so cheaply that some ranchers didn't bother to brand their young horses and let them run free, further populating the wild bands.

The British government sent representatives to ten western states to purchase horses. Buying stations were established at Miles City, Montana; Cheyenne and Sheridan, Wyoming; and Denver, Colorado. The British were willing to pay forty dollars per head for horses that were five to nine years of age. That seemed like a small fortune to ranchers, who hadn't been able to sell horses at any price. Horses were shipped to the buying stations from all over the west. Some were domestic ranch horses that had been recaptured after having been allowed to run free. Others were mustangs that were captured in the wild. Still others were saddle horses from cash-strapped ranches.

Because the horses were supposed to be broken to ride, cowboys drifted to the buying centers and offered to break horses for two to three dollars per head.

Export statistics show that in 1900 some 64,722 horses were exported from the United States. In 1901 the number was 82,250, and in 1902 when the Boer War ended, the number had risen to 103,020. While the British hadn't purchased all of these horses, they were major players in the export game.

Western horses participated in the Spanish-American War in 1898. The horses and riders receiving the most notoriety in this engagement were Teddy Roosevelt's Rough Riders. The Rough Riders were volunteers who came from all walks of life and from all over the United States. Most had two things in common: they could ride and they could shoot. There were many more volunteers than could be accepted, with about 1,000 chosen for the special regiment and undergoing training in San Antonio, Texas.

Roosevelt in his memoirs had this to say, in part, about the Rough Riders horses: "Meanwhile we were purchasing horses. Judging from what I saw, I do not think that we got heavy enough animals, and of those purchased, certainly a half were nearly unbroken. It was no easy matter to handle them on the picket-lines and to provide for feeding and watering; and the efforts to shoe and ride them were at first productive of much vigorous excitement. Of course those that were wild from the range had to be thrown and tied down before they could be shod.

"Half of the horses of the regiment bucked, or possessed some other of the amiable weaknesses incident to horse life on the great ranches, but we had abundance of men who were utterly unmoved by any antic a horse might commit. Every animal was speedily mastered, though a large number remained to the end mounts upon upon which an ordinary rider would have felt uncomfortable."

Roosevelt said his personal horses were purchased for him by a friend in Texas and that "...the animals were not showy, but they were tough and hardy and answered my purpose well."

Ironically, when the Rough Riders were shipped to Cuba where they and Roosevelt made the celebrated charge up San Juan Hill, their horses, except for the officers' mounts, were left behind in Florida and they fought on foot.

The horse that Roosevelt rode in the charge was named Little Texas. Roosevelt wrote that he stayed aboard Little Texas throughout the charge until about forty yards from the top of San Juan Hill. At that point he encountered a wire fence, dismounted, and turned Little Texas loose.

In World War I, western horses were called upon once again to serve; hauling artillery caissons and supply wagons, as well as being cavalry mounts.

Before it ended, World War I had dug deeply into the American equine reservoir. Between 1914 and 1916, the United States exported 357,553 horses to Europe for its allies, in addition to supplying its own

army. Rapid-firing machine guns took a heavy toll on horses of both sides in World War I. Estimates of horses killed in the conflict reach the several-million mark.

Deciding to create its own supply, the Army in 1910 established three breeding stations stocked with high-quality stallions and mares. Eleven years later, the U.S. Army created the Remount Service, a branch of the Quartermaster Corps. The Army, faced with a limited supply of horses due to heavy battlefield losses, had decided that it was too chancy to depend on purchasing horses at-large and would, instead, encourage breeders in various parts of the country to raise horses suitable for the cavalry. The irony is that by this time horses were no longer needed to wage war. The Army pursued its plan nevertheless.

The Army purchased Thoroughbred, Arabian, and Morgan stallions and placed them at remount

A U.S. Army Remount Depot.

stations in horse-breeding areas. By 1940 the Army was standing 644 Thoroughbred stallions, eighteen Morgans, and seventeen Arabians. Horse owners were urged to take their mares to these stallions, with the Army assuring, but not guaranteeing, them that it would purchase the offspring. Many western-type mares were taken to the remount stallions, once again mixing up the gene pool even further.

An army remount horse being shown for a "Parade of Horses" in Front Royal, Virginia.

World War II served notice that the horse was obsolete in battle, replaced by tanks, jeeps, and armored vehicles; the remount stations were closed.

The last recorded cavalry charge occurred in the Philippines on January 16, 1942, as Americans forces fought to prevent the Japanese from capturing Bataan. The charge was led by Edwin Price Ramsey and consisted of twenty-seven mounted members of the 26th Cavalry Platoon. They charged headlong into an advance guard of Japanese infantry and artillery, firing pistols as they rode. The Americans carried the day, but eventually the Philippines fell to the Japanese.

When one considers the millions of horses that died in combat, most of them anonymous in name and breeding, it seems only fitting that the last horse to be issued to the army by the quartermaster and the last to carry the U.S. brand also had an unknown pedigree. His name was Black Jack, and he was foaled January 19, 1947. His parentage was unknown, but he was a beautiful black gelding who was named after General John J. "Black Jack" Pershing, who was the supreme commander of American forces in World War I. The gelding was sent from Fort Reno in Oklahoma to Fort Meyer, near Arlington, Virginia, at the age of six. He became a part of the Third Infantry (The Old Guard) at Fort Meyer. For much of his career in the army, Black Jack served as a caparisoned (riderless) horse in funeral processions, as well as being involved in other ceremonial functions of the military.

Americans who are old enough likely will remember watching on television as an animated Black Jack pranced along behind the coffin of President John F. Kennedy in the funeral procession, saddle empty, reversed boots in place in the stirrups. Among the many other funeral processions in which Black Jack took part were those for presidents Herbert Hoover and Lyndon Johnson, as well as General Douglas MacArthur.

Black Jack died February 6, 1976, at the age of twenty-nine. His ashes were placed in an urn at a monument to him at Fort Meyer.

Black Jack's death served as the final punctuation mark to the end of the horse's role in war.

The Western Horse in Competition

10

As America became more mechanized, emphasis switched from breeding utilitarian horses to generating show ring or rodeo competitors. For years a western horse's worth was pretty much determined by his speed. While racing still remained popular, owners of non-racing western horses focused on their animals' other abilities, such as remaining calm and quiet and quickly responding to a rider's commands.

Interestingly, some of the show ring and arena activities that renewed interest in the western horse were those once performed on the open range, such as cutting and working cow horse. Other show ring events, such as halter, tested conformation or looks, while others, such as western pleasure and trail, developed to illustrate how horses handled everyday tasks.

But for capturing the feel of the range, nothing has topped cutting, one of the western-horse world's most popular and lucrative events. Cutting is also the basis for several other disciplines. Good cutting horses are suitable for reining and working cow horse events. The majority of winning reining, snaffle bit futurity, and working cow horses have pedigrees that contain cutting horse blood.

Cutting on the open range developed during roundups when cowboys would gather cattle into large groups. Most of the cowboys would ride around the herd to prevent cattle from wandering away. Meanwhile, a top hand from one of the ranches would enter the herd on a well-broke, quiet horse and ease out the animals that belonged to his employer, one at a time, to form a smaller herd.

Even back then, cowboys took pride in having a horse that could sort without spooking the herd. As corrals replaced loosely held herds on the open range, the need for a good "sorting" horse faded. However, riders who knew the thrill of working a good horse within a group of cattle would not allow that particular part of ranch work to disappear. Soon, weekend cutting competitions were being held in Texas, which remains the prime hotbed for the sport today.

The first recorded cutting horse event was held in 1898 in Haskell, Texas. Twelve horses competed for $150 in prize money.

The National Cutting Horse Association (NCHA) was formed in 1946 by a group of cowboys and ranchers at the Southwestern Exposition and Fat Stock Show in Fort Worth, Texas. Fifty-four members joined that year. Today, the association has more than 12,000 members in the United States and around the world and almost 120 affiliates.

Before long, the weekend cutters were looking for a signature competition for their sport and the crop of young horses coming up. The NCHA decided that the signature event should be a futurity for three-year-olds that had been nominated in advance, but who had never competed for prize money. The first NCHA Futurity was held in Sweetwater, Texas, in 1962, and thirty-six horses competed for the $18,375 in prize money. It wasn't long before Futurity prize money topped a million dollars. To enter a futurity, owners must pay the nomination and entry fees by certain deadlines. Horses nominated meet each December in Fort Worth and work through elimination rounds until only about twenty finalists are left. Winning championship, or even finishing among the top ten, greatly enhances a horse's value.

Today, hundreds try to qualify for a championship run. The Futurity now includes classes for amateurs, non-professionals, and professionals.

Cutting competition is structured, with rigid rules that provide penalties for mistakes and high marks for a job well done. The goals of a modern-day cutting competition differ from the "sorting" that cowboys did on the open plains. The old-time cowboy focused only on removing a cow from the herd and placing it into another group of bovines owned by his employer.

The modern cutter wants to show off his horse. Helpers pressure the cow back toward the herd to give the horse a chance to demonstrate its ability. The cutter's prime goal, while showing the horse to its best advantage, is to prevent the cow from re-entering the herd by darting into her path, no matter where she goes. "Losing a cow" — allowing her to re-enter the herd — is a major penalty and can cost the cutter five points.

Horse and cutter also are rated on how quietly they enter the herd and how well they isolate one individual without unduly disturbing the rest of the cattle, an ability highly regarded in the early-day sorting horse.

Judges sit above the arena and determine the degree of difficulty for the horse and how well it responded. At the Futurity at Fort Worth each year, five judges score the competition, with the high score and the low score thrown out and the three middle scores totaled for each cutter.

As the number of NCHA members and competitors have grown, so have the classes being offered. The organization held the first World Series of cutting, the NCHA World Championship Finals, in 1962. Conducted after the points for the year are totaled, the top fifteen horses and riders in the open and non-professional divisions are invited to the finals. Their points from the year, coupled with money won at the finals, determine who will be named World Champions.

As aficionados learned more about the sport, they found that horses from certain bloodlines excelled at cutting. Owners and trainers soon figured out that cutting horses can't be made. They have to be born with the instinct.

If they aren't born with "cow" sense, no one can

Intense concentration is required of both the cutting horse and rider.

train it into them. However, just as with hunting dogs, an astute trainer can help hone a cutting horse's skills if the instinct already exists.

Just how and why that innate ability surfaced in some bloodlines and not others is a mystery. But through selective breeding it is showing up more. The rule of thumb is that breeding a stallion with cutting horse instincts to a mare with the same instincts is likely to produce an offspring with cutting horse instincts.

And while most of the stellar cutting horses of today are Quarter Horses, that doesn't mean they are the only ones with the cutting instinct. In fact, one of the great progenitors of the modern-day Quarter Horse, the Thoroughbred stallion Three Bars, was said to amuse himself when penned with cattle by sorting one and moving it around the pen or corral.

So strong is this instinct in some horses that they will cut anything that moves in front of them, be it a cow, a person, or a flag that flits back and forth on a movable string. All that is needed to set them in motion is movement and a signal from the rider.

Many of the competitive western horses of today are specialists. If a horse is a cutter, it often competes in no other classes. The same is true of horses involved in reining, working cow horse, and roping or team penning competitions, though there are exceptions.

It hasn't always been this way. When the workaday world for the horse gave way to the competition arena, many horses were asked to be versatile. They might be judged on conformation one day; be involved in western pleasure the next; and perhaps be entered in a cutting event or in a race the day after that.

The change in the western horse's moving from "Mr. Everything" to specialist can best be demonstrated by Doc Bar, one of cutting's leading progenitors.

Doc Bar

Doc Bar, foaled in 1956, was the grandson of the highly acclaimed Thoroughbred runner Three Bars,

and the son of Lightning Bar, whose successful racing career was cut short by injury.

Doc Bar's dam, Dandy Doll, had racing credentials, too. She had gone to post twenty-one times and had finished first five times, second twice, and third three times. She also had a magnificent pedigree, being a daughter of Texas Dandy, who was a son of the great racing sire My Texas Dandy.

With all of the genetic ammunition ready to fire, the gun jammed. Doc Bar was a complete bust as a racehorse, earning less than one hundred dollars in his brief career. He started four times with nary a win, and he barely escaped being last in his final race, finishing nine lengths behind the winner.

Though small, Doc Bar was a very handsome colt. He apparently inherited his good looks from his sire, Lightning Bar, who was a halter champion in addition to being a stellar racehorse and a top-notch sire.

In later years as his fame and stature grew, rumors circulated in the western equine world that Arabian blood was responsible for Doc Bar's fine head and body. He also carried a fair amount of Thoroughbred blood. All Thoroughbreds' lineage traces to the three Arabian or Barb imports, and Doc Bar traces through his Thoroughbred side to the Darley Arabian.

Doc Bar was bred by Jim Finley's Finley Ranches in Gilbert, Arizona. Finley's horse-raising operation produced both racehorses and all-around ranch horses. Finley named the tiny sorrel colt "Doc Bar" to honor his stepfather — affectionately known as "Doc" Gooden — and the colt's sire, Lightning Bar.

When Doc Bar failed so abjectly as a racehorse, Finley decided as a last recourse to show him at halter, even though he didn't possess the muscular "bulldog" conformation popular with judges at the time.

Finley turned Doc Bar over to trainer Charley Araujo of California, who was known for picking potential winners at both halter and performance and then fitting and showing them to championship status. Araujo was successful in turning Doc Bar into a halter champion, but not before unsuccessfully trying to turn the little stallion into a reining horse. Doc Bar couldn't, or wouldn't, get the hang of it.

However, halter competition produced a different result. The compact little horse with exquisite facial features turned the heads of judges, and soon they were looking his direction and away from the larger, heavier-framed horses that had been winning.

Araujo campaigned Doc Bar seriously from 1960 through 1962, during which time Doc Bar won nine Grand Championships and one Reserve Championship, along with twelve first-place victories, all in prestigious shows. Those wins translated into thirty-six AQHA halter points, which are awarded for wins.

But, that wasn't all. Araujo had also convinced the Finleys to let him breed the stallion, and the stallion's offspring were also garnering titles. At Doc Bar's final show, he was named Grand Champion at the Cow Palace in San Francisco. One of his sons, Barlet, was Reserve Champion Stallion, and a daughter, Janie Bar, was Reserve Champion Mare. In addition, his progeny won the Get of Sire competition.

In 1962 Araujo put Doc Bar in full-time stud duty. Doc Bar's offspring continued to succeed for a time, but then the fickle nature of halter showing reared its head. The small, pretty Doc Bar horses were beginning to fade from favor in lieu of taller, more muscular animals.

However, bigger and better things were looming on the horizon for the offspring of Doc Bar and Poco Bueno, the stallion who had fostered the "in" bulldog look in the pre-Doc Bar halter days.

Poco Lena

Poco Lena, a well-bred daughter of Poco Bueno and the mare Sheilwin, was foaled at the famed Waggoner Ranch in Texas, which owned Poco Bueno. In addition to being a talented cutting horse, Poco Lena also won at halter and performance in AQHA-sanctioned shows.

Owned and trained by Don Dodge, Poco Lena won World Champion Cutting Mare honors three times and was Reserve World Champion five times. She was so talented that she won not only under an excellent rider in Dodge, but also with B.A. Skipper, an amateur who needed a seat belt to stay aboard.

In 1962, the year Doc Bar retired from the show ring, Skipper, who had purchased the mare from Dodge, won aboard Poco Lena at a cutting competition in Douglas,

Doc Bar enjoyed enormous success in the show ring.

Arizona. After the contest, his private plane crashed on the way home to Texas and Skipper was killed.

Poco Lena and another mare were being sent back to Skipper's ranch in Texas by trailer. Somehow, in the aftermath of Skipper's death, the two of them were forgotten and remained on the trailer without food or water for five days. The other mare recovered, but Poco Lena, who already had a history of foot problems, foundered badly.

In the same year that Poco Lena foundered, Doc Bar, now six years of age, was purchased from the Finleys by Dr. and Mrs. Stephen Jensen of California. The couple started their horse careers in the halter show ring but later ended up breeding some of the best cutting horses in the country. They moved in that direction when Skipper's widow held a dispersal sale that included Poco Lena. Though crippled by founder and unable to perform, the great mare still commanded a winning bid of $14,200.

After the sale, a dispute erupted between buyer and seller. Mrs. Jensen, learning of the disagreement, stepped in and offered to buy Poco Lena. She was taken up on the offer, and the mare was trucked to her new California home to be bred to Doc Bar. Suffering from founder and having been subjected to hormonal treatment for years to prevent her from cycling during the show season, Poco Lena appeared unable to come into season, let alone become pregnant.

But in 1967, at the age of eighteen, she gave birth to her first foal, later named Doc O'Lena, on the Jensens' front lawn. The Jensens had turned over their front lawn to Poco Lena so that the cushiony surface would be comfortable for her painful feet.

The next year she again got in foal to Doc Bar and produced another colt, also born on the Jensen's front lawn. This one was named Dry Doc. It wasn't long after Dry Doc was weaned that Poco Lena was euthanized. Poco Lena was later inducted into the NCHA Hall of Fame.

Doc O'Lena

Doc O'Lena was the first of the two brothers to solidify Poco Lena's legacy and establish Doc Bar as the horse to breed to in the cutting horse world.

Ridden by Shorty Freeman in the 1970 NCHA Futurity, Doc O'Lena won the championship after being the only horse ever to win every go-round, including the semi-finals and finals.

A year later, his brother, Dry Doc, also won the NCHA Futurity and was ridden to victory by the now legendary trainer Buster Welch.

These two young stallions were not the first of Doc Bar's get to win in the cutting pen, but they were

Poco Lena was a multi-talented competitor.

the two that firmly established him as a top progenitor in the sport.

Leo San

The crossing of Doc Bar with a Poco Bueno daughter had stellar results in the show arena. But so did the crossing of the bloodlines that produced Leo San. On the top side, he was a son of Leo, who traced back to Joe Reed II and Joe Reed, two significant stallions whose progeny won on the track and in the halter and performance show rings. On the bottom side, Leo San traced back in one line to Zantanon, the sire of King who, in turn, sired Poco Bueno.

A wealthy Texas oilman named Gordon B. "Jimmy" Howell owned Leo San. Howell's goal was to raise outstanding horses that not only could do it all in western riding, but also were pleasing to the eye. Leo San sired many offspring, two of the very best being brothers. Their mother, Peppy Bell, traced back on the top side of her pedigree to Old Sorrel, the foundation sire at King Ranch in Texas.

The first-born, Peppy San, won many cutting championships, ridden to a number of them by Matlock Rose, a premier cutting horse trainer. Peppy San was three in 1962, the first year the NCHA Futurity was held. He finished second, beaten by one point.

In 1967, again with Rose in the saddle, Peppy San won the NCHA World Championship. Peppy San stood at stud at Rose's facility but still kept competing. In the 1967 Tournament of Champions held in Vernal, Utah, Peppy San won the championship in

six tough rounds of competition.

The following year, Peppy San was ranked third in AQHA high-point open cutting and finished the season as the AQHA high-point cutting stallion. He wound up his career in 1968 with Rose's wife at the time, Carol, riding Peppy San to second in the non-pro division of the NCHA World Championship Finals.

At stud, Peppy San was a huge success, siring numerous winners. One of his offspring would weld the Leo San line to the Doc Bar line.

Peppy San's brother was Mr. San Peppy. Ridden and owned by Buster Welch, the gritty stallion won one championship after another, including the 1974 and 1976 NCHA World Champion Cutting Horse Finals, becoming one of only three two-time winners in the history of cutting. However, one of his greatest achievements was being the sire of Peppy San Badger, often called Little Peppy, who did what his sire didn't — win the Futurity Championship.

Smart Little Lena

It is only natural that eventually the great sire lines of Leo San and Doc Bar would be joined

Smart Little Lena had extraordinary cow smarts.

through their descendants. That intermingling occurred between Doc O'Lena, the Doc Bar son, and Smart Peppy, a granddaughter of Leo San. (She was a daughter of Peppy San.) The diminutive colt that was the product of this union was Smart Little Lena.

Born in 1979, the scrawny little colt, bred by Hanes Chatham of Pilot Point, Texas, was described as being no bigger than a German shepherd. Chatham waited until the colt was twenty-five-months old before he got on him. (Futurity prospects often are started under saddle when less than two calendar years of age.)

Chatham had a feeling that this colt was something special, so he sent him to a neighbor, Bill Freeman, for some finishing work. The little colt's ability when put on cattle impressed Freeman, one of the top cutting horse trainers in the business and the son of Shorty Freeman.

Chatham had consigned Smart Little Lena to a sale, but withdrew him and gave Freeman the green light to train and show the colt in the Futurity. That wasn't enough for Freeman. He sold all of his cattle and some syndicate shares in Smart Little Lena to raise the money to purchase a half-interest in him.

Just three months before the Futurity, Smart Little Lena and another Futurity colt at Freeman's training center ingested some blister-beetle-infested hay and became very ill. The other colt died, and Smart Little Lena just barely survived.

He recovered completely, though, and at the 1982 Futurity, he and Freeman swept the opening two rounds, finished second in the semi-finals by one point, and then came back to win the championship. His score at the finals was 225, at the time the highest score ever awarded to a cutting horse at the Futurity.

Smart Little Lena was not finished. He captured the 1983 Super Stakes and tied for the 1983 Derby title, making him the first NCHA Triple Crown winner. He was retired to stud about a year later with earnings that totaled $743,275.

His sons and daughters have also been success-ful, both in the show ring and the sale ring. Smart Little Lena's offspring have earned in the ten-million-dollar range, and his foals and descendants continue to bring top dollar at prestigious cutting horse sales.

And, as with racing, astute breeders researched pedigrees and came up with some marvelous combinations, such as crossing a son of Doc Bar on a granddaughter of Leo San to get a remarkable horse like Smart Little Lena.

His bloodlines and those of Doc Bar also have produced champions in the western disciplines of working cow horse competition and reining.

Working Cow Horse and Reining

In working cow horse competition, the horse stops, turns, and drives the cow through a prescribed pattern.

Two of the leading sires of working cow horse champions in recent years have been Smart Chic Olena and Nu Cash. Smart Chic Olena is a son of Smart Little Lena. Nu Cash was sired by the great cutting stallion Colonel Freckles and is out of a Doc Bar granddaughter.

The racing influence has been gradually weeded out in horses bred for cutting, working cow horse, and reining, though there are exceptions. One such exception is Miss N Cash, a stallion who earned a grand total of $124,662 in his cutting career. Doc Bar-bred on the bottom of the pedigree, he is the son of the great racing sire Dash For Cash, a grandson of the Thoroughbred stallion Rocket Bar.

However, it is much more common today to trace the lineage of cutters, reiners, and working cow horses back three or four generations without coming into contact with what is considered racing blood.

While cutting and working cow horse competition involves cattle, reining does not. In reining, the horse is judged on its ability to run through a prescribed pattern.

The horse must negotiate flying changes of lead while doing a figure-8, do sliding stops, and demon-

The sliding stop, one of reining's most spectacular moves.

strate balance, athletic ability, and speed with spins.

One of the most notable horses whose pedigree is not synonymous with "established" cutting horses of today is a handsome dun named Hollywood Dun It, who stands at Tim McQuay Stables in Tioga, Texas. Hollywood Dun It was sired by Hollywood Jac 86 out of a mare named Blossom Berry, by Dun Berry. In 1986 Hollywood Dun It won Reserve Championship honors in the National Reining Horse Association Championship and the following year won the Derby and Superstakes, two of the most prestigious events in the world of reining.

However, his breeding is the exception rather than the rule. The majority of successful reining horses carry heavy doses of cutting horse blood.

While most of Hollywood Dun It's pedigree features non-cutters, there is a connection with one of the great cutting horse progenitors. Hollywood Dun It's sire, Hollywood Jac 86, was sired by Easter King and Easter King was sired by King, the sire of Poco Bueno.

Hollywood Dun It has been as successful in the breeding barn as he was in the show ring and has become the first reining stallion whose descendants have won in excess of two million dollars.

The Western Horse in Rodeo

11

odeo traces back to the heyday of the true cowboy on the open range. During roundups, cowboys were likely as proud of a good roping horse as a good sorting horse. It isn't hard to imagine cowboys wagering who among them could out-rope all comers.

It must be remembered that the horses ridden by cowboys in the 1860s and 1870s did not have the benefit of a training program. "Training," for them, frequently consisted of being roped and tied to a solid post in the center of a corral, then having a saddle put on and a cowboy climbing aboard.

These horses were often first saddled at age four or older. Prior to being "broke," their only contact with man was being roped and if a stallion, castrated. Thus, these horses had developed an independent nature and a fear and dislike of being restrained. They were as wild as their ancestors, and they posed a serious challenge to a ranch's bronc buster, the cowboy charged with breaking these horses.

The bronc buster's approach involved little finesse. While his assistants restrained the horse with ropes and a blindfold, the bronc buster climbed aboard. The horse was then set free, and it was a battle to the finish. If the cowboy stayed on until the horse was exhausted and unable to continue bucking, he was well on his way to victory. If, however, he was thrown, the bronco came back even tougher the second time around.

After two or three such sessions, the horse usu-

ally submitted to being saddled and mounted without always bucking. However, with this rudimentary handling and training, the horse often remained on the "broncy" side, looking for any excuse, especially early-morning cold, to cut loose with a fit of bucking.

Paintings by Charlie Russell and other western artists, along with songs like "The Strawberry Roan," depict such episodes as a horse bucking out of control, sometimes through the morning cooking fire, and the cowboy trying to ride him out. Horses that became adept at dislodging riders couldn't be used as ranch horses.

Saddle bronc competition started in the latter 1800s when cowboys or ranchers would take a serious bucker to a roundup and wager that no cowboy present could stay on the horse.

In those early days, horses were not bred to be buckers, but because of the way they were raised and the temperament some possessed, they fought rather than submit. Today, rodeo contractors breed horses with what they hope will be the power and inclination to buck. If the desire and ability are there, these horses wind up in a rodeo bucking string; if not, they are broken as saddle horses.

Rodeo

From informal weekend contests, rodeos have grown into organized events usually held before thousands of spectators.

The Rodeo Association of America formed in the

1920s as a loosely organized group that included rodeo committees and promoters. During those early days, the committees and promoters pretty much made the rules, and cowboys often competed for meager paydays and under the scrutiny of sometimes-questionable judges.

Feeling exploited, rodeo competitors organized the Cowboys Turtle Association in 1936. They named themselves such because they were slow to act but had finally stuck out their necks for their cause. The name remained until 1945 when it was changed to the Rodeo Cowboys Association. Some thirty years later "Professional" was added to the beginning of the title, making it the PRCA.

Today, the association has more than eleven thousand members and sanctions more than seven hundred rodeos throughout the United States and Canada.

The PRCA plays an even more important role as far as the animals and contestants are concerned — regulating and policing the sport. With mounting pressure from animal-activist groups, the PRCA is sensitive to the issue of animal welfare and has instituted a number of rules and regulations requiring humane treatment of all rodeo animals.

The signature event for the PRCA each year is the National Finals Rodeo (NFR), which is held in Las Vegas. While cowboys once rode for pocket change, today's elite contenders compete for hundreds of thousands of dollars. More than four million dollars is awarded at the finals rodeo alone. Competing for the purse are the top fifteen cowboys in each rough stock event (saddle bronc, bareback riding, and bull riding) and timed events (team roping, calf roping, and steer wrestling), along with the top fifteen women money earners in barrel racing.

The horses that carry these cowboys and cowgirls to the pay window are extremely valuable. Contractors who furnish the livestock for rodeos will pay thousands of dollars for a bucking horse that can highlight a prestigious rodeo. On the other hand, cowboys who are lucky enough to have an exceptional roping horse simply don't sell it.

Saddle Bronc Riding

Saddle bronc riding remains rodeo's premier event. It carries the mystique of the Old West with man pitted against outlaw horse.

The bronc rider must have strength and, more importantly, style, grace, and precise timing. All of the rider's moves must be synchronized with those of the horse, and the rider must stay aboard the horse for eight seconds. During that time he is allowed one hand on a bucking rein attached to the horse's halter. His free hand must not touch the horse, himself, or the saddle during the ride.

The rider must also have the heels of both feet in front of the point of the horse's shoulders when it is turned out of the gate. If he does not, the judges will rule that the rider "missed him out" and disqualify him.

To stimulate the horse to buck higher and harder, a strap is placed over the flanks and in front of the rear legs. While the flank strap is an irritant that helps stimulate vigorous bucking, PRCA officials are quick to say that it does not inflict pain. If it were pulled painfully tight, they point out, the horse would refuse to buck at all. When a horse feels serious abdominal pain, its inclination is to lie down and roll about, not buck.

PRCA rules dictate that the flank strap must be covered with sheepskin and have no sharp objects protruding. It can be pulled snug when the horse leaves the bucking chute and must be immediately removed, using a quick-release buckle, by a pickup rider when the eight-second whistle blows.

Two judges usually score the contest. By combining their scores, based on how hard the horse bucked and how well the cowboy rode, one hundred points is possible if everything is "perfect." Scores usually range from the seventies to the eighties, sometimes reaching the nineties.

At the turn of the twentieth century, the event was more like bronc breaking at the ranch.

Early rodeos had no bucking chutes. The saddle-bronc rider would lead his horse into the arena and saddle it. Because many of the broncs were untamed, two assistants held and blindfolded the horse, just like at the ranch.

Once the cowboy saddled the bronc, he climbed aboard, gripping two reins attached to a hackamore. His assistants then turned the horse loose, and if a cowboy were to be successful, he had to ride the horse to a standstill.

The early bronc riders were not required to exhibit any spurring action, but they could not grab the saddle horn and hang on. For a time, spurs were barred from saddle bronc riding, partly because some cowboys were using them to help stay aboard. Promoters banned the spurs, believing that staying on without them would be more difficult. Later, as the rules and approach to riding and judging changed, spurs were again allowed as long as they were blunt and the rowels rolled easily so that they could not be jammed into a horse's hide.

To obtain a high score and remain aboard a bucking saddle bronc, riders must synchronize spurring action with bucking action. The highest-rated spurring action begins with the rider's feet far for-

ward on the horse's shoulders and then sweeping back to the cantle as the horse bucks or kicks out with its rear legs. The rider then snaps his feet back to the horse's neck a split second before the front feet hit the ground.

As rodeo grew more popular, saddle bronc riding underwent more changes. No longer was the horse led into the arena and saddled. Bucking horses were placed in chutes, where they were saddled and the

Saddle bronc riding is rodeo's premier event and harks back to the Old West.

cowboy could ease onto the horse's back and decide just where he wanted to grip the bucking rein.

In the beginning, the broncs used were anything that couldn't be ridden at the ranch. In some cases, a cowboy would arrive at a rodeo with his own bucking horse in tow.

At the beginning of the twentieth century, a bronc named Steamboat became the prototype for high-scoring bucking action.

Steamboat also became an icon for Wyoming, where he was foaled in 1896 near Chugwater. His bucking was so extreme that, in addition to drawing fans, it drew filmmakers and photographers. A 1903 photograph by University of Wyoming professor B.C. Buffum showed Steamboat being ridden by Guy Holt, one of the few cowboys to ride the horse to a standstill. Due to the intense bucking action shown in the photograph, Steamboat is most likely the horse shown on the University of Wyoming's logo, though another popular bucking horse, Deadman, is a possibility. Regardless, the bucking horse symbol has become synonymous with Wyoming. Since 1936, a bucking horse and rider has appeared on Wyoming license plates in homage to rodeo horses and the cowboy legacy of toughness and spirit.

In addition, a fourteen-foot-high sculpture of Steamboat being ridden by a cowboy who represents the men who rode or tried to ride him was dedicated at the University of Wyoming in 1990 as part of the state's centennial celebration.

Steamboat's sire was a Percheron, and his dam was a mare from Mexico that likely carried blood that traced back to horses the conquistadors brought over. Steamboat was coal black with three white socks — both rear feet and the right front. His powerful body and rather large head demonstrated his Percheron blood. His athleticism and quickness descended from his dam's family line.

He received his name while being castrated as a three-year-old. When the cowboys threw him to the ground, the youngster's head struck the hard earth with such force that a bone in his nose broke. From then on, he whistled like a steamboat when he breathed.

As was the custom in those days, Steamboat was turned out to pasture after being gelded. In the spring of his four-year-old year, the cowboys set about breaking him and other young prospects as saddle horses. The black colt would have none of it. He preferred bucking off cowboys.

By the time Steamboat was five, he had pretty much deterred most cowboys attempting to ride him. John Coble, a rodeo contractor who was looking for some bucking horses, ended up buying him for less than fifty dollars.

Unlike many of the bucking "outlaws" of the day, Steamboat was easy to handle on the ground. Normally, he would even stand quietly in the arena while being saddled. However, once the cowboy climbed aboard, the horse turned into a stiff-legged, whirling dervish. He was ridden a few times, but not often.

Early in his career, Steamboat was purchased by Charlie Irwin, who, along with his brother, Frank, operated a Wild West Show and also provided bucking stock for the Cheyenne Frontier Days in Cheyenne, Wyoming. In 1907 and 1908, Steamboat was named the Worst Bucking Horse of the Year at Frontier Days. He might have won the title more frequently had it been given away for more than just two years. Steamboat remained a featured bucker at Frontier Days through 1912, after which Irwin lost the contract for providing rough stock. From then until his death two years later, Steamboat starred in Irwin's Wild West Show.

As part of Irwin's show, a twenty-five-dollar reward was offered to anyone who could ride Steamboat. If no one showed up to accept the challenge, Irwin would have one of his own cowboys try to ride the horse.

Unfortunately, Steamboat was fatally injured in 1914 after a show in Salt Lake City. The bucking horses had been penned when a storm hit. Frightened, the horses began dashing around, and in the melee, Steamboat severely cut himself on the wire fencing. He was sent home to Wyoming, but serious infection set in, and he was destroyed with a single rifle shot to the head.

Because Steamboat was gelded at age three, he left no offspring to carry on his bucking ability. However, bucking-horse breeders of today are combining the same general bloodlines that produced Steamboat. The cross combines draft horses with more hot-blooded equines, such as Thoroughbreds.

This isn't to say that all great saddle broncs are big. A prime example of a talented but smaller saddle bronc is Five Minutes to Midnight, who was also coal black. He weighed barely nine hundred pounds and was featured at rodeos, including Frontier Days, from 1929 through 1945. During those sixteen years, only five cowboys were able to ride him.

Early on, he was teamed with another black bucker named Midnight. This horse had a large, heavily muscled frame and weighed more than twelve hundred pounds, like Steamboat. Midnight bucked off riders with sheer power while Five Minutes to Midnight relied on cunning and quick, catlike moves. Midnight was easy to handle and even appeared in Cheyenne Frontier Days parades at the end of a lead line. Five Minutes to Midnight, on the other hand, had no time for people and was difficult to handle. Midnight was retired in 1933 after a relatively brief career that was shortened by foot prob-

Bareback bronc riding is the most physically demanding of rodeo events.

lems, but Five Minutes to Midnight kept bucking for another dozen years.

Both are buried on the grounds of the Cowboy Hall of Fame in Oklahoma City.

Bareback Bronc Riding

A rodeo event that does not trace to the range is bareback bronc riding. It is strictly an arena event. No old-time cowboy would ever think of climbing on a horse without a saddle or reins attached to a halter, bridle, or hackamore.

That being said, many cowboys declare bareback bronc riding the most physically demanding event in rodeo. According to the PRCA, bareback riders endure more abuse, suffer more injuries, and carry away more longtime damage to their bodies than all other rodeo cowboys.

A bareback rider can use only a leather rigging that is placed atop the horse's withers and tightened into place with a cinch. With one hand wedged firmly into the rigging's suitcase-like handle, the rider nods to signal that the gate is to be opened.

When the horse comes flying out into the arena, the rider must have both spurs in front of the horse's shoulders until the animal's front feet hit the ground. As the horse bucks, the rider pulls his knees up, dragging his spurs up the horse's shoulders. As the horse descends, the cowboy straightens his legs, returning his spurs over the point of the horse's shoulders in anticipation of the next buck.

A bareback rider is judged on his spurring technique, the horse's ability to buck, the rider's ability to keep his toes turned out during the ride, and his all-around good form in staying aboard for eight seconds.

Many of the top bareback bucking horses will never be ridden in saddle-bronc competition, or the converse, because these horses have been bred and developed to specialize. The saddle bronc tends to be a bigger, more heavily muscled animal, while the bareback horse is more slender, but a bit quicker and more agile.

Team Roping

Team roping events are reminiscent of life on the open range. One cowboy, called the header, ropes the steer around the neck or horns. His or her partner, called the heeler, ropes the animal's heels.

This skill was a necessity on the open range. When a cow, steer, or bull had to be doctored for an ailment, such as hoof rot or pinkeye, and only two cowboys were present, one would "head" and the other "heel" the animal, stretching it out on the ground. Their horses were trained to keep tension on the ropes while the cowboys dismounted

and tended to the bovine. When finished, the cowboys would remount and shake free their loops. They did not want to be afoot when removing the ropes because the doctored animal often had lost all of its good humor.

In the rodeo arena, the steer is roped in a similar fashion, only now speed is of the essence. A skilled pair of ropers can head and heel a steer in five seconds or less.

Some specific rules apply. First, the steer is allowed a head start. A barrier is stretched across the chute in front of the header. It is released when the steer reaches a predetermined point. As the barrier is released, the two cowboys charge forward, the header in the lead and the heeler trailing. If the header charges forward too quickly and breaks the barrier before it is released, the team is penalized ten seconds.

Team roping requires speed and strength of the horses competing in this event.

Calf roping has its origins on the open range.

The header ropes first and must make one of three legal catches on the steer — the rope must be around the horns, around one horn and the head, or around the neck. Any other catch is illegal, resulting in disqualification.

After the header makes the catch, the steer is turned to the left, so that the heeler can rope both hind feet. If the heeler catches one foot instead of two, the team is penalized five seconds. In top-notch PRCA competition, a penalty of any kind often takes a team out of contention for prize money. The clock continues running until the two cowboys turn their horses and face each other with no slack in their ropes.

As with other competitive equine events, the horses used for team roping have been specifically bred. The header's horse tends to be taller and more heavily built so it will have the power to turn the steer after it is roped.

Both heading and heeling horses must be fast in order to carry the roper quickly to the correct position. It also takes several years to train a good roping horse, and many are able to compete into their sen-

ior years. One Champion team roper, Blair Burk, competed in the National Finals Rodeo on a twenty-eight-year-old horse.

The PRCA has responded to humane concerns in team roping by requiring that rebar (metal) and plaster be placed around the horns of roping cattle prior to a contest, and to prevent rope burn, that all steers be fitted with horn wraps that extend four inches down the jaw from the base of the horns.

Calf Roping

Calf roping is another rodeo event that originated on the open range. In the early days a sick calf was lassoed and held by the roping horse while the rider dismounted, pulled the calf off its feet, and held it on the ground while he doctored it.

Calves also were, and still are, roped at branding time on ranches, though a different approach is employed. The calf is roped around the back feet and dragged to a crew that will flatten it on the ground so that it can be branded, castrated, dehorned, and vaccinated.

99

As with team roping, the cowboy on the range or in the branding pen works quickly, but without undue haste. Not so in the rodeo arena. Speed is crucial.

Once again, a barrier is placed in front of the roper so that the calf gets a head start. Once the calf reaches a predetermined point, dependent on the length of the arena, the barrier is released and the roper can advance. An athletic, speedy horse is needed, as well as an athletic, speedy roper. The horse must come out of the roping box at full speed and quickly close the distance between the roper and the calf. The roper then throws a loop around the calf's neck. This is the signal for the horse to slide to a stop, bringing the calf to a halt.

The roper bails off the right side of the horse, runs to the calf, flanks it to the ground, and ties three feet together with a "piggin' string." The cowboy then remounts and rides his horse several steps so that there is slack in the rope. A judge with a stopwatch studies the calf for six seconds. If the calf kicks free from the tie, the roper is disqualified. If the calf remains tied, the time is valid.

Teamwork between roper and horse is paramount. Once the calf is roped and on the ground, the horse must keep tension on the rope but not pull back so hard that the calf is dragged along the ground. Under PRCA rules, calves used in roping events must be healthy and weigh between 220 and 280 pounds.

Once again, we are dealing with horses that often are specialists. As is the case with team-roping horses, it normally takes several years to turn out good calf-roping horses, and their value increases with their ability.

Ropers tend to select a horse based on conformation and temperament rather than pedigree and then seek to develop it into a willing and winning contestant. Temperament, the top ropers say, plays a significant role. These horses must withstand miles and miles in the trailer and still remain sound and healthy. They must also stay calm and relaxed in a roping box while surrounded by hundreds or thousands of noisy people in the stands. Yet, in a split second, they must go from standing quietly to racing full speed down the arena after a calf or steer.

Good steer-wrestling horses have to be fearless and fast.

Steer Wrestling or Bulldogging

As with bareback bronc riding, steer wrestling (or bulldogging, as it once was known) does not have its roots in ranch life. Born as an entertainment event, steer wrestling has since developed into an important part of rodeo that also requires specialist horses. Steer wrestling used to be a novelty event in which a cowboy used his teeth on the steer's nose to bring it to earth.

Bill Pickett, a black cowboy, pioneered the event. He learned the technique from watching a dog sink its teeth into the upper lip of a steer and hang on. In pain, the steer sank to the ground. Pickett first employed the technique on the Texas ranch where he was born and grew up. He later demonstrated it in the rodeo arena, usually as part of the Miller 101 Wild West Show in the early 1900s.

During Pickett's performance, a "hazer" rode alongside the steer to keep it running in a straight line. Pickett would range up along the other side on his horse, leap onto the steer's back, grip it by the horns, and twist its head until he could sink his teeth into its upper lip or nose. He'd then throw his arms wide and topple off the steer's back. The combination of the man's weight and the pain from being bitten on the nose caused the animal to fall on its side. Pickett performed his act for some years at venues across the country and around the world.

However, it was obvious from the beginning that this was not going to be a sport that would be permitted in rodeo. For one thing, it was inhumane and, for another, not too many cowboys were willing to bite a steer in the nose or upper lip. Instead, they turned the event into steer wrestling. As with the roping events, the steer is given a head start, with the steer wrestler and his horse remaining behind the barrier. Once the barrier is released, the wrestler dashes after the steer. A hazer on the other side attempts to keep the animal running in a straight line.

As the wrestler comes up alongside the steer, he leans over and slides from his horse, grasping the steer by the horns. He digs in with his boot heels, bringing the steer to a stop. By putting one hand under the steer's chin and the other on a horn, along with correct timing, the wrestler exerts enough leverage to flip the steer onto its side.

The gifted steer wrestler, mounted on a fast and

In PRCA rodeos, women compete exclusively in barrel racing, but the event is fun and challenging for both sexes and all ages.

courageous horse, can put a steer on its side in as few as three seconds or less. In fact, the world record is 2.4 seconds.

Excellent steer-wrestling horses are not easy to find. The steer wrestler's horse must be exceptionally quick out of the starting box and must have the courage to race right up beside the steer's tossing horns and have the instinct and training to run on once the wrestler leaves its back.

Often, the owner of a good steer-wrestling horse and a good hazing horse can make money by renting them to other contestants. In return, the horse owner receives twenty-five percent of the wrestler's winnings in the event.

Barrel Racing

At PRCA rodeos, barrel racing is strictly limited

to women, though men compete in non-PRCA barrel racing.

So tough is the competition at major barrel-racing contests that time must be measured to within a hundredth of a second with an automatic timer to determine winners.

The contestants race in a cloverleaf pattern around three barrels. The goal is to travel the cloverleaf course at speed, but to avoid knocking down a barrel. When a barrel is knocked over, the rider is assessed a ten-second penalty, pretty much eliminating her chances at the pay window.

These horses, too, are specialists. Often, the successful barrel racer will have Thoroughbred blood running through its veins. It must have the athletic ability to turn sharply around each barrel and the speed to cover the straightaway distance from the last barrel to the time line in scant seconds.

Pickup Horses

The pickup men are an integral part of any rodeo. It is their job to race into the arena once a saddle bronc or bareback ride is finished, help the rider dismount, and remove the flank strap.

Their horses, too, have become specialists. Generally they weigh between one thousand pounds and twelve hundred pounds. They must have the courage and speed to race up beside a horse that is bucking and kicking and still have the strength to maintain course while the bronc rider grabs the pick-

up man around the waist and either swings himself over the back of the pickup horse or to the ground and safety. At the same time, pickup horses must be strong enough to handle a two-thousand-pound bull on the end of the lariat if that animal decides it doesn't want to leave the arena after its eight seconds of action in the bull-riding event.

Rodeo's Influence

Rodeo has had a strong influence on the development of specialists within the western horse world. Though all of the specialists fall into the western horse category, there are differences as to type and conformation based on the event. A heading horse, for example, often will be larger and more powerful than the heeling horse — more of the solidly built and powerful Joe Hancock look. A calf-roping horse will be smaller than a heading horse but extremely quick and agile. The barrel-racing horse, often carrying Thoroughbred blood, will tend to be a bit more refined, with a body that is muscular enough to power it around the barrels in tight turns at speed and yet light boned enough to make a flying dash from the final barrel to the finish line.

Rodeo has also influenced the western horse temperament. These competitive animals must be calm enough to stand quietly behind a barrier while the calf or steer gets a head start and yet have the competitive desire to blast out of the box at full speed at the cowboy's signal.

The Western Horse in Fiction and the Movies   12

The era of the cowboy endured only about twenty years, but the cowboy of the Old West gained immortality in fiction, radio, television, and the movies. So did the cowboy's horse, which media transformed from a working animal to a companion with almost human traits.

This portrayal influenced the public's perception of the western horse, especially the casual owner who was seeking a trail-riding mount and family companion. When these people went shopping for a horse, they wanted one that looked like what they had seen and read about; a horse that was strong enough to carry them, gentle enough that it wouldn't buck them off, and one that would respond to kind ministrations. Movies helped popularize the "look" of the western horse — the Quarter Horse, Appaloosa, and Paint.

The romanticizing of the cowboy and his horse began as the era of the open range and cattle-driving cowboy was ending in the 1880s. The new image started with Buffalo Bill Cody, who had never herded cattle in his life. However he was a celebrated frontier scout, winner of the Medal of Honor for fighting the Cheyenne, Pony Express rider, and buffalo hunter, among other things.

His life began verging on legend when an author using the name Ned Buntline wrote *Buffalo Bill, King of the Border Men*. Ultimately, Buffalo Bill's life would be the subject of 550 dime novels.

After being immortalized in fiction, Buffalo Bill himself took to the stage in 1872 in plays that toured eastern cities. During his travels, Cody recognized that easterners craved to know more about the west. They were fascinated by, and, perhaps, a little frightened of life in the West with its open spaces, adventures, outlaws, and what they perceived to be bands of renegade Native Americans.

Cody decided to capitalize on this fascination and formed a Wild West Show that took to the road in 1883. The show featured a little bit of everything — cowboys, homesteaders, mounted cavalry, Native Americans, sharpshooters, stagecoaches, and trick riders.

Cody was a consummate showman, and he knew his audience. He once attended a New York ball in white tie and tails and a large white Stetson hat. It was Cody who invented the high-crowned ten-gallon hat, which the Stetson company made to his specifications. He grew his hair long and wore a moustache and beard because, he said, he would not be believable as a scout otherwise. Often he wore buckskin clothing with long fringes and knee-high boots.

His rather flamboyant attire would inspire the cowboy movie actors who followed in his wake.

The "cowboys" in Cody's show rode broncs, buffaloes, and bucking bulls to prove their ability and came to the rescue when outlaws robbed the stagecoach. Audiences loved it, and Cody decided to push the cowboy image even more. He chose a cowhand named William Levi "Buck" Taylor to be billed as

"King of the Cowboys." Taylor was well suited for the role. He was born in Texas and had been on trail drives to Kansas. While little that he did as part of the show resembled what he had really done as an authentic cowboy, Taylor came to symbolize the public's perception of a cowboy.

Taylor became so popular that in 1887 a dime novel, *Buck Taylor, King of the Cowboys*, portrayed him as a cowboy hero who rode forth with six-shooters strapped to his hips. While the real-life Taylor was a good hand with horses and understood cattle, the fictional Taylor had little need for those skills. Instead, he was a tough fighter, a deadly shot, and an excellent rider. He was also a decent man who fought only on the side of right.

The short novel was a huge success. Hundreds and hundreds of stories about cowboy heroes followed, changing their image forever, thanks to the seminal efforts of Buffalo Bill Cody.

Horses in Cody's shows did more than just carry cowboys, cavalry, and whooping Native Americans into battle. A number of the horses were trained in precision movements, while others were schooled to dance or jump through hoops of fire. As was the case with Cody's garb, his use of horses would be emulated a few years later in the movies.

Cody loved horses and was an excellent rider. His first horse was a sorrel stallion named Prince that his father obtained in a trade with Native Americans in the Kansas Territory. Buffalo Bill, whose full name was William Frederick Cody, was born near Davenport, Iowa, but his family moved to the Kansas Territory in 1854. Cody rode dozens of horses for the short-lived Pony Express in 1860 and 1861. While hunting buffalo, he often rode a horse named Brigham, the fastest horse he said he had ever owned.

Cody's favorite mount in later years was a big white gelding named Isham that he rode in the Wild West Show. A photo taken of Cody shows him on a white horse, believed to be Isham, that appears to be at least part Thoroughbred but might also have had

some Arabian, Saddlebred, or maybe even old-line Chickasaw blood. Isham, it appears, represented the emerging western horse with its variety of bloodlines.

Cody was known for his generosity. When Sioux leader Sitting Bull, who traveled with the show in 1885, took a liking to a particular gray "dancing" horse in the troupe, Cody gave the horse to him. Four years later, Sitting Bull was shot to death by members of his own Lakota tribe at his home on the Standing Rock Reservation in the Dakotas. As the first shots rang out, the gray horse must have taken them as a cue to perform and began dancing.

In 1902, the same year that Cody took his show to Europe for a four-year stint, Owen Wister further glamorized the cowboy in his book, *The Virginian*. The Virginian was a cowboy whose name was not used in the book. He was a strong, quiet man, virtuous, loyal, and in love with a schoolteacher. *The Virginian* would provide the blueprint for plots in later western books and films and be the basis for several movies and a television series of the same title.

The movies that first appeared around the turn of the century had no sound, and dialogue and descriptions of what was happening were flashed across the screen in subtitles. One of the first westerns of significance was the 1903 movie *The Great Train Robbery*, although the movie was shot in New Jersey instead of the West. A number of early westerns were shot in the East, using fake backdrops. It would be at least ten years into the twentieth century before the movie industry began its move to California.

The Great Train Robbery which had little to do with cowboys, was based on the exploits of western train robbers such as Jesse James and the Wild Bunch. However, a series of films glorifying the cowboy followed. He no longer appeared as merely a cattle drover and horseman; instead he became something of a latter-day Sir Gallahad, righting wrongs and doing it with flair and gusto while decked out in gaudy chaps, silver spurs, and a ten-gallon hat.

The movie-going public met this new hero with open arms. The industrial era had arrived with its stifling factories and assembly lines, and many working-class citizens were looking for diversion from the daily grind. Horses galloping across the silver screen carrying gun-toting cowboys conveyed action and excitement and provided a wonderful form of escapism.

Early films concentrated more on the cowboy than they did his horse, but that would change. One of the first actors to pay special attention to his horse was W.S. Hart, who had been a classical actor on the New York stage, but at age forty-nine switched to western movies. He debuted in 1900 and continued making westerns for twenty-six years.

Hart rode a pinto named Fritz, and he would often be filmed scratching and petting his and others' mounts to demonstrate his great affection for horses. Soon Fritz was also getting top billing on movie posters.

Hart, who was a screenwriter as well as actor, became a student of the cowboy and insisted on its accurate portrayal. His costumes, for example, were low key. Nevertheless, Hart's films still pitted good against evil with good winning out, often under the influence of a loving woman.

Tom Mix, a former rodeo rider, soldier, and lawman, had no use for the conservative approach when he came on the scene in 1910.

He wore a ten-gallon hat and colorful shirts. Silver adorned his horses' saddles, bridles, and breast collars. He also promoted the publishing of embellished stories about his past, further enhancing his image as a real western hero.

Mix, perhaps more than anyone else, established the horse as a companion and an integral part of the early westerns. His first screen mount, Old Blue, was quickly replaced by a younger horse named Tony.

Olive Stokes Mix, who was married to the flamboyant actor from 1909 to 1917 and wrote his biography, *The Fabulous Tom Mix*, said a friend found Tony, then a colt, tied to a horse-drawn chicken cart travel-ing down a street in an Arizona town. Mix later bought Tony from his friend as a two-year-old.

Although Olive Stokes Mix described Tony as looking like a Thoroughbred, Tony appears in photos to be more Morgan. (Some accounts report that Tony was a Morgan and was raised on a Texas ranch. His sire is listed as a stallion named Headlight Morgan. How the colt wound up tied to a chicken cart in Arizona is not explained.)

Tony became immensely popular as Mix hit full stride in the silent movie era of the 1920s. Mix was a lithe, athletic man and did all of his own movie stunts. Many of them involved Tony, but some of the more dangerous ones featured a horse named Buster that looked like Tony.

Mix taught Tony some twenty tricks, ranging from untying a rope to dancing, bowing, lying down, counting, nodding, shaking his head, and rearing on his back legs. When Tony first began appearing in movies in 1914, the public loved him and sent him almost as much fan mail as Mix. When Mix went on tour, Tony traveled in his private railway car and Mix in his.

Both Mix and his horse were fearless in their stunts, one of which nearly killed them. A dynamite explosion in one scene was to go off just after Mix and Tony rode over the spot where the charge was set. Movie production officials urged Mix to use a double and another for Tony because of the inherent danger. Mix refused. Disaster struck when the man setting off the charge miscalculated, and the blast went off when Mix and Tony were on top of it. The two were buried in the rubble.

Olive Stokes Mix related in her book that Tony lay quietly until Mix was freed and only then struggled to his feet. The horse suffered a gash in his side but recovered and was soon back in front of the cameras. Before his career ended, Mix had starred in 336 films, most of them also featuring Tony. No one other than Mix trained or rode the horse, according to Olive Stokes Mix.

In the late stages of his career, Mix acquired

Tom Mix, aboard one of his stunt horses, became a silent film star renowned for his bravura.

only played the role of modern-day knight but strummed his guitar and sang as well.

Gene Autry, who made his movie debut in 1935, was perhaps the most famous singing cowboy. Autry's flashy attire outdid even Mix. His shirts featured colorful embroidery, and his trousers sometimes were decked out with silver conchos. He carried two pearl-handled pistols, and his gun belt was adorned with silver, as were his saddle, bridle, and the breast collar of his horse. His equine companion was a liver chestnut named Champion. The original Champion is described in some accounts as being a Morgan. He had a big blaze and three white socks. He came from a ranch in the Ardmore, Oklahoma, area, not far from where Autry grew up. The horse would be only one of many Champions that Autry rode through a career spanning two decades.

Like Tony, Autry's Champions were taught a variety of tricks. One of Autry's signature moves would come at a climactic point in the movie when he would run up behind a standing Champion and leap over the horse's rump into the saddle. Champion would be off and running at full speed just as Autry hit the saddle.

Tony Jr., a horse who looked like the original Tony, but was not related. While the original Tony had two white rear socks and a blaze, Tony Jr. had four white socks and a blaze. Little is known about Tony Jr.'s pedigree.

As his movie career wound down, Mix formed his own circus and toured with it, featuring Tony in his act.

The original Tony died in 1942 at the age of thirty-two, two years after Mix died in a one-car accident on an Arizona highway. Sadly, the horse that had received tons of fan mail at his peak died in anonymity. There is no record of if or where he was buried.

By the 1930s, movies had added sound and were the rage, especially westerns. The cowboy hero not

The original Champion was Autry's mount from 1935 until the actor went into the armed services in 1942. When the war ended and Autry resumed his acting career, another Champion became his movie mount. Originally named Boots, Champion Jr. looked a lot like the original and was described as being a Tennessee Walker. Autry purchased Champion Jr. for $2,500 from an Ada, Oklahoma, rancher named Charles Auten when the horse was four. Champion Jr. appeared in his first movie, *Sioux City Sue*, in 1946.

Autry's most famous contemporary was Roy Rogers, who was born in Ohio as Leonard Slye. One of Rogers' signature garments was a fringed buckskin jacket, and he sometimes wore white gauntlets that reached almost to the elbow. He also had a silver-bedecked gun belt and wore a white hat. He rode a Palomino horse named Trigger. As with Autry and Champion, the original Trigger would be only one of many Palominos ridden by Rogers and his stunt doubles. However, Rogers' heart would hold a special place for Trigger.

Rogers and Trigger appeared in their first western feature, *Under Western Stars*, in 1938. Trigger was registered as Golden Cloud. His sire was a Thoroughbred that had raced at Agua Caliente racetrack in Mexico, and his dam was a Palomino. The original Trigger was foaled on a small ranch near San Diego that singer Bing Crosby owned in part.

When Trigger was three he was sold to Hudkins Stables where he was trained by renowned horse trainer Glenn Randall, who later would train the black Arabian, Cass Ole, of *The Black Stallion* fame. Trigger first appeared in the movies as the mount for Olivia de Haviland when she starred with Errol Flynn in *Adventures of Robin Hood*.

The original Trigger died at age thirty-three in 1965, and Rogers had the horse stuffed and displayed in his California museum. (The museum has since been moved to Branson, Missouri.) The stuffed Trigger is positioned rearing

on his back legs, a move often featured at the close of a Roy Rogers movie.

Both Autry and Rogers, and their horses, successfully moved into television with their careers extending into the mid-1950s.

Another still-famous cowboy and his horse made their television debut in 1949. Clayton Moore portrayed a masked doer of good deeds, The Lone Ranger. He rode a white stallion named Silver. Jay Silverheels portrayed his Native American sidekick, Tonto, who rode a Paint named Scout.

The Lone Ranger got its start in 1933 on radio where actor Bruce Beemer read the lead role. However, when program owner George W. Trendle

Gene Autry, "The Singing Cowboy," and his horse Champion were matinee idols.

moved the program to television, Beemer was deemed a bit hefty for the new medium. Trendle instead chose the tall, handsome, and athletic Moore to play the role.

Moore reportedly picked the first Silver, whose name had been White Cloud. Trendle purchased him from the Hooker horse ranch in California's San Fernando Valley. Silver stood seventeen hands, and though Moore maintained he was a Morab — half Arabian and half Morgan — wranglers on the set claimed that the horse was really a Tennessee Walker. Based on Silver's size, one would be inclined to side with the wranglers.

Silver, twelve at the time and a calm, placid horse, readily took to his role.

Trendle purchased Silver #2 as a four-year-old in 1949. The horse reportedly was half Arabian and half Saddlebred. Moore, however, maintained that the

second Silver also was a Morab. This Silver's disposition was opposite that of the original's. Instead of being calm and sedate, he was excitable and high strung. Glenn Randall was called in to train the second Silver. By 1952, Randall declared that his protégé was ready for the cameras. Because of the horse's excitable nature, he often was used for the action scenes, and the original Silver was brought out when the script called for Silver to be standing still, calm, and relaxed. Still other Silvers filled in when stuntmen took over some of the dangerous scenes.

However, Moore insisted he be the one riding Silver as the horse reared and The Lone Ranger waved at the cameras or the audience. Once, when on tour and performing at a North Carolina fairgrounds, Silver #2 slipped on wet grass while rearing and toppled over on Moore, who wasn't seriously hurt but suffered a leg injury that kept him on

Roy Rogers and Trigger reinforced the idea of the cowboy as hero and the horse as best friend.

crutches for a couple of weeks.

Hopalong Cassidy's white horse, Topper, also gained fans among television viewers. Had the show stuck to the book's story line, then that probably would not have been the case. Writer Clarence Mulford's Hopalong Cassidy was a hard-bitten man who limped because of an old bullet wound — thus his name. He was a working cowboy who drank too much, talked too much, and chewed tobacco. The Hopalong from Mulford's book rode a mean and ugly horse named Red Eagle who tried to throw his rider at every opportunity. For his transgressions, the fictional Red Eagle would earn a serious verbal dressing down.

Of course, the Hopalong portrayed on television and in the movies by William (Bill) Boyd was the opposite. He had blond hair, always dressed in black, used neither tobacco nor alcohol, and was ready to do battle for good at the drop of a ten-gallon hat.

Horses in the movies caused almost as much stir as the actors around them. Whenever singing cowboy Eddie Dean found himself a new mount, a press release introduced the horse prior to the movie's release. And Dean, like his on-screen cowboy counterparts, had no qualms about changing horses and was beholden to no particular breed. His first horse was a Paint named War Paint; his second a dark-colored horse named Flash. His third was a Palomino he raised and trained on his ranch. His final screen mount was named Copper and was described as being a Quarter Horse.

Jimmy Wakely, a cowboy actor in the 1940s, rode a horse named Lucky for three years. Then, inexplicably, he gave the horse away as a prize on the radio program *Queen For A Day*.

His studio announced shortly thereafter that Wakely had found the new mount he'd been looking for. The horse of his dreams had four white feet and a bright, rich color. That was all the information the studio proffered, but the movie-going public had been served notice that the star would be on a new

horse in his next movie.

No matter what the movie or television show, though, all of the horses were portrayed as being strong, kind, and intelligent. They were companions and partners rather than utilitarian as they had been for the real cowboy.

As the 1950s wore on, the careers of the wholesome singing cowboys and their horses wound down. In their place appeared a new kind of cowboy. In many cases, this newcomer still was a good guy battling evil, but he had a flaw or at least a shady background.

Subtly, as these new characters forged their way into America's living rooms, the horse began to lose his individual character. The action scenes were more exciting than ever, but the horse became little more than a prop.

One new TV series after another cropped up in the 1950s and beyond. The public's appetite for westerns seemed insatiable. Among the popular shows were *Bonanza*, about a widowed father and his three good-yet-dissimilar sons' cowboy exploits on the Nevada rangeland; *Rawhide*, about trail drives from Texas north; *Gunsmoke*, about a cow-town marshal and his efforts to maintain law and order; and *Have Gun — Will Travel*, about a wandering gunfighter named Paladin whose catch phrase was the show's title.

For the most part, horses were anonymous in these westerns. Ben Cartwright always seemed to ride a Buckskin that appeared to be of Quarter Horse lineage in *Bonanza*, while Little Joe always piloted a black and white Pinto that looked as though it might have some Arabian blood, and Hoss sat astride a big black that appeared to be of mixed blood that might even include some draft horse. Yet these horses rarely were referred to by name, and their roles, generally speaking, were to get the human actors from one point to another.

When James Arness rode a horse in the long-running *Gunsmoke*, it was usually a Buckskin of Quarter Horse extraction that appeared too small for the actor's big frame. Arness was awkward in the saddle.

This, too, was a change from the cowboys of the earlier era. Though the singing cowboys might have looked like duded up caricatures of real cowboys, most of them could ride and seemed at ease in the saddle. Not so with the new generation of actors. Many of them looked completely out of place on a horse.

As westerns focused more on the cowboy than the horse their portrayals became more unrealistic. For example, the western hero of the screen generally was handy with his fists and quick on the draw. The real cowboy likely was neither. True, he packed a gun, but he used it primarily for killing rattlesnakes, putting down a seriously injured animal, or shooting into the air to slow or divert stampeding longhorns. Trail-weary drovers also shot off their pistols in jubilation as they rode down the streets at the end of a trail drive — sort of like fireworks on the Fourth of July.

Then, too, the early pistols weren't all that accurate and many were rather clumsy to handle, making it difficult to whip one from the holster and hit even a stationary target. Gunfighters with skill, accuracy, speed, and finesse undoubtedly existed, but the average cowboy certainly wasn't one of them.

It also seems unlikely that the early cowboy engaged in fistfights. First of all, he spent most of his time in the saddle and would have no way of being proficient with his fists. Second, he made his living with his hands. A cowboy that got into a bare-knuckle battle was risking his livelihood. It's pretty hard to throw a loop or take a dally (wrap the rope around the saddle horn) if your hands are beaten up or broken.

Then, there are the films starring actors like Clint Eastwood that turned the cowboy into a wanderer. Often the main character would show up at a ranch or town with little or no explanation as to where he had been or what he had been doing. He would simply come riding in, a small bedroll tied behind the cantle of his saddle.

Jack Schaefer's *Shane*, which was both a book and movie, epitomized this type of cowboy. The hero comes riding up to a Wyoming homestead and hangs around to help clear some land. You know from the start that Shane is a gunman, but nothing reveals where he has been or what he has been doing — just that he has been wandering throughout the West and now appears ready to hang up his gun.

Eventually, he joins the homesteaders in a stand against a cattle baron though almost no scenes involve cattle or cowboys herding them on horseback. It is a classic western with its big fistfight and a climactic gunfight, after which the mysterious Shane, slightly wounded shooting down the villains, rides away. We can only guess where he is going and what he will be doing. Throughout, horses are just there for transportation.

A more recent book that was made into a movie, *All The Pretty Horses*, rekindled in its pages and on the screen a cowboy's appreciation for his horses, something most modern westerns have ignored. The story, by author Cormac McCarthy, takes place in 1949, a time when one could still travel cross-country from Texas to Mexico by horseback. The main character, John Grady Cole, loves horses and has an innate ability to train them. He even puts his life on the line to retrieve horses that have been taken from him. Most of the horses in the movie are "western" horses.

Unfortunately for western movie and horse buffs, many of the early western movie stars and producers weren't concerned about a horse's pedigree or background. They were only interested in whether the horse looked right for the part and whether its temperament fit the actor who would ride it. As a result, much of the information concerning the background of certain early movie horses has been gleaned from information passed down by people who have recollections of the horses rather than from documented evidence.

Problems Facing the Western Horse

13

Through the efforts of dedicated owners, the western horse has overcome inbreeding, war, man's greed, and near extinction to thrive in today's world.

During the Civil War alone, thousands of well-bred horses were killed in action. Entire bloodlines were wiped out. In the late 1870s the army destroyed thousands of Appaloosas during conflicts with the Nez Perce Indians.

The wholesale slaughter of thousands of wild horses most assuredly included quality animals. True, unfettered reproduction had resulted in a great many stunted and inferior horses, but many good horses were caught in the same net of destruction.

Through it all, though, devoted horse owners continued to upgrade the western horse. The goal was to produce a better horse, which, to some, meant one that could run faster than its contemporaries. To others, it meant a horse superior at cutting, reining, roping, or western pleasure. The list goes on.

While man did much to produce a better horse, he also made some inappropriate decisions. Some of the "mistakes" were deliberate. The unfortunate fact is that not everything done to the horse in the name of progress has been beneficial.

Man has repeatedly placed his own economic needs at the forefront. Many times breeding decisions have been based more on the whims of fashion in the marketplace than on improving a particular strain, bloodline, or breed. If a particular bloodline is popular in the sales arena, many breeders will capitalize on it, even though they know the cross is inappropriate for their stallion or mare. The breeders will profit, but the new owner might find the resulting horse incapable of performing as anticipated.

Economics and fads have influenced more decisions in racing and halter showing than in other equine disciplines.

Through it all, the western horse has persevered, despite man's sometimes-misguided interference.

Halter Showing

Halter showing was originally intended as an event to pick a breed's best representatives based on conformation and to set a standard for breeders.

But there was more to halter showing than just looking nice at the end of a lead shank. When the event first began in the early 1900s, a halter horse was also expected to be a performance horse, maybe racing one day and competing in a pleasure class the next.

Before long, however, the halter horse became the poster boy for the breed, without having to perform in any other events. The halter show ring would, and still does, create fads with particular looks coming in and out of style.

Two examples are the stallions Poco Bueno and Doc Bar, though they both are from the era in which halter horses were also expected to perform.

The king of the halter ring before Doc Bar was

Poco Bueno, a compact, solidly built stallion. Some breeders called it the "bulldog" look, and at the time it was the winning standard for the Quarter Horse breed. Foaled in 1944, Poco Bueno was a son of foundation sire King. Both sides of his pedigree traced to the legendary Traveler. Poco Bueno lived until 1969 and had twenty-four foal crops with 405 foals registered by the AQHA.

As a sire he set new standards in performance as well as in halter. His progeny included 163 halter-point earners and 118 performance-point earners. Along the way he sired thirty-six AQHA Champions, eighty-four Performance Registers of Merit, twenty-one Superior Halter Awards, and thirteen Superior Performance Awards. Great as those accomplishments were, they weren't enough to keep the Poco Bueno look at the forefront in the halter ring.

Doc Bar, foaled in 1956, set a new standard for halter horses that called for them to be smaller, more refined, and a bit prettier. That look held sway for several years, and Doc Bar was a popular halter stallion. Then fashion changed again. Larger horses once again headed for the winner's circle in halter competition, while the smaller Doc Bar-types were relegated to "also ran" status.

Another era in halter showing arrived with Impressive, who carried some of the same blood as Doc Bar. He was taller than Doc Bar and Poco Bueno and was exceptionally handsome with well-defined muscles. He was foaled in 1969, the same year Poco Bueno died.

Impressive set the new standard for halter horses in the stock horse breeds, but he also brought an unwanted genetic flaw.

Impressive was by Lucky Bar, a son of the Thoroughbred Three Bars. Impressive's dam, Glamour Bars, was a daughter of the Three Bars' stallion Lightning Bar, sire of Doc Bar. On the bottom side of Glamour Bars' pedigree was another son of Three Bars — Sugar Bars. Thus, Impressive is closely inbred to Three Bars.

Impressive wasted little time in setting new stan-

In halter competition, the ideal can depend on prevailing tastes.

dards for halter competition. He won thirty-one first-place ribbons in as many shows. Early in his career, he was sold for twenty thousand dollars. Three months later his new owners resold him, doubling his price to forty thousand dollars.

His fame grew when he was named World Champion Senior Stallion. His success as a stallion was as phenomenal as his success in the show ring. Of the top fifteen halter horses in 1992, thirteen descended from Impressive.

His statistics glowed throughout his breeding career. Even at the age of twenty-five, Impressive was fourth on the list of top-producing stallions. During his long tenure as a premier breeding stallion, he sired more than two thousand offspring. It was estimated in 1993 that the pedigrees of more than 55,500 Quarter Horses, Paints, and Appaloosas around the world included Impressive.

Unfortunately, while his sons, daughters, and grand-get were winning at halter and other competitive events, some suffered episodes of muscle twitching that often left them temporarily unable to move. At first veterinarians and owners alike thought the horses were either tying up or suffering from colic. Yet, the afflicted horses didn't seem to respond to colic treatment.

In 1992 researchers at the University of California, Davis, developed a diagnostic DNA blood test that can detect what is now known as hyperkalemic periodic paralysis (HYPP), a genetic disorder. These sporadic attacks of muscle tremors, such as shaking or trembling, weakness, and even collapse, can be accompanied by paralysis of the muscles of the upper airway, causing loud breathing. Occasionally, a severe paralytic attack can cause sudden death, presumably from heart failure or respira-

Impressive had a successful show career but is most often associated with the genetic disorder HYPP.

tory muscle paralysis.

A report authored by veterinarian Sharon Spiers, one of the lead researchers at Davis, gave this explanation of the condition:

"In horses with HYPP, studies revealed a defect affecting a protein called the voltage-gaited sodium channel, a tiny gateway in the membrane of muscle cells. This gateway controls the movement of sodium particles in and out of the muscle cell. These sodium particles carry a charge that changes the voltage current of the muscle cell, allowing it to contract or relax. In horses with HYPP, the regulation of particles through the sodium channel occasionally fails, disrupting the normal flow of ions in and out of the muscle cell, causing uncontrollable muscle twitching or complete muscle failure."

Researchers from Davis decided to find out whether HYPP was heritable. They first bred a stallion carrying the gene to an affected mare. Three embryos were harvested from the mare, resulting in the births of three offspring — two colts and one filly. All three were afflicted with HYPP. Researchers believed the condition to be heritable, but they wanted to know beyond a doubt, so they conducted a second trial.

An affected stallion was bred to eleven unaffected mares of various breeds. At the same time, three affected mares were bred to an unaffected stallion. With the help of embryo transfer, the breedings resulted in seventeen foals. All seventeen youngsters were tested for HYPP at two months of age. The tests revealed that ten were affected with HYPP. This result proved beyond a doubt that HYPP is a dominant genetic trait.

Because HYPP is a dominant trait, the researchers reported, the breeding of an affected mare or stallion to a normal horse results in an approximately fifty percent chance of the offspring carrying the trait. If two affected horses are bred, there is at least a seventy-five percent chance the foals will be affected. The good news is that the breeding of a normal offspring from an affected horse to another normal horse will result in normal offspring.

Because HYPP is a dominant gene, it can cross breed lines, meaning that it isn't restricted to Quarter Horses.

But then came the bombshell that all of the horses diagnosed with HYPP traced to Impressive.

Thousands of horses descended from this great stallion, and they represented a dollar value in the millions.

Perhaps because of concern about the turmoil that would be created, Impressive's identity as the source of the mutant gene was not immediately revealed. Then, in late fall 1993 at a meeting of the American Association of Equine Practitioners, Spiers gave a talk on HYPP. During a question-and-answer session, she was asked if the condition was restricted to a single bloodline. She said, "yes."

"What was the bloodline?" she was asked.

"Impressive."

Now the word was out, and the AQHA was in the midst of political upheaval. What steps should it take? True, horses in other breeds carried the mutant gene, but only if they traced to Impressive, a registered Quarter Horse.

The AQHA registry handled the problem by requiring that the following notification be placed on the registration certificates of 1998 foals descending from any bloodline determined to carry the HYPP gene (at this point Impressive was not named in the rule by AQHA): "This horse has an ancestor known to carry HYPP, designated under AQHA rules as a genetic defect. AQHA recommends testing to confirm presence or absence of this gene."

Next, the registry decided that beginning in 1999 all foals tracing to Impressive must be tested for HYPP and the results of the test affixed to the foal's registration papers. Foals from a sire and dam that had already tested negative for the condition would be exempt.

From there, it would be up to the breeders. If someone wished to breed to an affected horse, there would be no rule against it. However, the unspoken message was clear — the only way the condition can ultimately be eradicated is by breeding only unaffected horses.

Interestingly, it did not work out that way. Breeders continued to use the Impressive line, seemingly even more. Whereas the condition was spread inadvertently at the beginning, some breeders now seemed to be deliberately aiding and abetting the spread.

Veterinarian Jonathan M. Naylor, a researcher at the Western College of Veterinary Medicine, University of Saskatchewan, addressed this phenomenon in the *Canadian Veterinary Journal* in 1994. He pointed out that many breeders, indeed, were breeding for HYPP-positive horses. The reason, he said, was because HYPP horses tended to produce bulging muscles and that was the prevailing look in the show ring.

AQHA registry officials say they do not have data to substantiate or refute the statements Naylor made in the 1994 *Veterinary Journal* article. However, they do say that breeders continue to breed affected horses. Some of them, they said, are gambling that the gene won't be expressed, noting the fifty percent chance that the horse will not be affected if only one parent is affected. Of course, the odds go up to seventy-five percent if both parents are affected. In gambling parlance, these breeders are "rolling the dice." Others, perhaps, accept the possibility that the mutant gene will be expressed, but they think that the condition can be treated with medication and diet if it does crop up. Still others see an opportunity in HYPP. If horses with HYPP present a more muscular look in the show ring, why not go for it? Forget what it does to the horse and that the condition is thereby perpetuated.

The breeding issue becomes somewhat confusing with both moral and economic questions. Is it morally justifiable to conduct a breeding program that could harm a breed? The economic question is more straightforward. What else does one do, for example, with a broodmare or stallion that has been purchased for thousands of dollars and is HYPP positive?

The true fancier of the western horse would probably answer that a short-term loss on the part of an individual or individuals would be better than long-term damage to an entire breed.

Unfortunately, HYPP is not the only debilitating malady attributed to Impressive.

Leg and Feet Problems

The quest to emulate Impressive's large, solid build and excellent conformation also has created other problems for halter horses. With or without involvement of his pedigree, breeders in pursuit of those qualities often have been responsible for producing horses with some definite weaknesses. The goal was to beget a sizable horse with massive muscles. Many times heavily muscled horses have been led into halter competition on legs that are too fine and feet that are too small to support the horse properly.

Horses so conformed, though attractive, perform few useful functions. Many are unable to withstand the rigors of ranch work, roping, or even trail riding.

Obviously, horses of this type are more prone to foot and leg problems.

Tying Up

While HYPP is a relatively new malady for the western horse, exertional rhabdomyolysis, or tying up, has been around for years. The affliction is similar to muscle cramps, only it can be much worse.

Tying up can take many forms. In the days when draft horses tilled fields and pulled freight wagons, the condition was often called "Monday morning disease" because it often struck draft horses that had been in harness all week but were idle on Sunday.

Horses tie up with varying severity. Some just appear to be stiff and reluctant to move, especially in the hindquarters. Others with a more severe form appear to be suffering from colic and may throw themselves to the ground in pain and agony from cramping muscles

One form of the condition is often seen when young, high-strung fillies are placed in a race training program. Researchers are trying to determine whether the tendency toward this form of tying up is heritable and more likely to occur in certain Thoroughbred bloodlines than in others, somewhat like HYPP being confined to a single bloodline. Often, this form of tying up will occur after vigorous exercise.

Still another form of the condition, which appears to show up primarily in quiet, muscular western horses, involves an abnormality in glycogen or glucose metabolism. The condition is called polysaccharide storage myopathy. Simply put, muscles store glycogen rather than converting it to energy, causing muscle cramps. The problem has shown up in Quarter Horses, Paints, Appaloosas, draft horses, draft crossbreds, warmbloods, and even a few Thoroughbreds. It often can be appropriately treated by regulating the horse's diet — no sweet feeds or grain, grass hay instead of alfalfa, and a fat supplement that takes the place of glycogen in providing energy.

Here again, heredity might be raising its head. In a joint study, researchers at the University of Minnesota and the University of California, Davis, identified twenty-three horses with polysaccharide storage myopathy. Of that number thirteen were Quarter Horses, four were Paints, three were Appaloosas, and three were Quarter Horse crossbreds. In the eighteen pedigrees available for these horses, three stallions figured prominently.

If research reveals that the tendency toward the condition is heritable, the solution will be the same as that for eradicating HYPP — not breeding horses likely to pass along the disorder.

A halter class being judged.

In both of the above cases, man was inadvertently involved in the early going. Hundreds of people infused Impressive blood into their western horse breeding programs because they wanted to produce the best horse possible. They had no way of knowing at that time that a harmful mutant gene might be a passenger. However, breeders now must accept responsibility for promulgating the condition if they breed affected horses.

Performance Horse Problems

While we might be quick to blame halter horses for the breed's problems, other disciplines are not exempt.

Many of the great cutting horses today contain the bloodlines of Doc Bar and Leo San, two stallions with the instinct to out-maneuver and outwit a bovine.

While line breeding (crossing horses of the same general family lines) and inbreeding (close-up crossing, such as breeding a stallion to his daughter) often accentuate a bloodline's positive traits, they can do the same with negative traits.

Too much of the same blood can yield horses with conformational weaknesses or defects, such as weak hocks in a cutting horse, that might predispose it to injury. The more line breeding and inbreeding that is involved, the more need there is for paying special attention to conformational defects when purchasing a performance horse or when selecting a stallion for breeding purposes.

Pleasure Horses

Similar inappropriate breeding decisions can be made in a discipline as non-stressful as western pleasure. As is the case with halter horses, pleasure classes often fall prey to the look or way of going popular at the time.

In many western pleasure classes, a horse with a low-hanging head and that minces along with short little steps is at the top of the hit parade. This is not a natural gait for most horses, but some breeders have solved this problem by breeding for horses with straighter shoulders and thus a shorter stride.

A horse with a straight shoulder will also have straighter pasterns and, as a result, will not have much shock-absorbing capability in the front legs. Horses with this type of conformation will be susceptible to foot and leg problems.

In western pleasure competition, horses keep their heads down and their stride short.

117

Accentuating Leg Problems

Man is also responsible for promulgating a number of leg problems, particularly in Thoroughbreds. This is important to the western horse because Thoroughbred blood is prevalent in racing Quarter Horses, Paints, and Appaloosas, as well as in breeds used in barrel racing.

Through the years the Thoroughbred has been bred for speed, often at the expense of good leg and foot conformation. Unfortunately, a great many young Thoroughbreds break down because of this before fully maturing. An example is the chestnut stallion Charismatic who won the 1999 Kentucky Derby and Preakness but broke down in the Belmont Stakes. The horse was three years old. He survived the injury but could no longer race. He was immediately retired to stud duty, and mare owners were soon standing in line to breed to him. The same thing has occurred with dozens of other racing Thoroughbreds in which owners have invested hundreds of thousands of dollars.

It is a matter of economics. The owner is attempting to recoup his or her investment, and when a well-bred horse breaks down, the breeding barn is the best way to do it. Unfortunately for the breed, the horse might have had a genetic defect that contributed to the breakdown. By putting a horse with such a genetic weakness into a breeding program, more horses with the same weakness or weaknesses will weaken the breed.

The Western Horse Today at Home and Abroad 14

A colorful history has followed the western horse into modern times and there is more to come. The western horse's ranks are growing steadily as more and more people in the United States and abroad grow to appreciate and enjoy this amazing animal.

Time has changed how we use the western horse, but even these modern-day uses retain links to the past. Though cowboys and their horses no longer face off with longhorn steers on the open range, rodeo and ranch work provide opportunities for the western horse to shine. And, while "quarter-paths" no longer cut through the southern and eastern woodlands, the genes of the horses that trod those paths continue to race today. And the descendants of horses that once helped settle America still hit the trails as the pastimes of trail and pleasure riding continue to grow.

The reasons for the continued popularity of the western horse are many and varied. A growing number of people are entering competitive equine events, both in this country and abroad. Team roping, for example, reigns in the western United States, while team penning is popular all across the county. Cutting and reining events continue to expand, and the same is true of barrel racing. Western horses are even involved in jumping, eventing, and dressage. And, one cannot forget the western horse continues to play a prominent role on western ranches. All of this tends to swell their ranks. However, the popular-ity of trail riding is the most significant reason more western horses are being bred.

Trail riding for pleasure began back when the horse was no longer needed for work. As people's leisure time and discretionary income grew, more and more discovered the horse and trail riding. Governmental agencies, assisted by trail riding enthusiasts like the Back Country Horsemen, con-structed trails on state and federal lands for horses. Stronger and better trucks and trailers are now on the market, providing transport to trails throughout the country.

All three of the mainstream western horse reg-istries — Quarter Horse, Paint, and Appaloosa — recognize the growing interest in trail riding and have adopted programs to promote more recreation-al riding among their members. Appaloosa owners, for example, can participate in a Chief Joseph Trail Ride each year. The ride covers a portion of the trail followed by the legendary Nez Perce chief and his band as they fled toward Canada. Both of the other registries also stage trail rides for members and offer special awards for riders who cover a certain number of miles trail riding.

A survey conducted by the American Paint Horse Association at the turn of the twenty-first century revealed that fifty percent of the APHA membership is primarily interested in recreational riding. As a result, the APHA decided to host member trail rides. The APHA had earlier implemented an innovative

Ride America saddle-log program. After signing-up with the program, riders keep track of their riding hours and become eligible for awards at various levels of achievement.

In addition, the APHA distributes a free *Guide to Recreational Riding* to all of its members. The thirty-six-page booklet is filled with tips for enjoying and caring for horses. The AQHA and Appaloosa registries also offer similar programs to encourage recreational riding.

While trail riding for pleasure is stimulating continued and growing interest in the western horse, many other horses are used much the same way as they were in the heyday of the cowboy. The big difference is that today's western ranch horse must share duties with four-wheelers, dirt bikes, and, of course, pickups and trailers.

Almost all ranches in the western United States maintain a saddle horse string or at least a few horses that can be used for roping and gathering cattle. In many cases, they are not used every day, but when they are needed, their services are highly valued.

In several western states, cattle are often "wintered" in valleys, where they give birth in the spring and are fed by the ranchers. Horses are sometimes used to check on prospective bovine mothers, much like they were in the day of the early cowboy. When ranchers come across a newborn, they can step down from the horse and punch an identification tag into the calf's ear, as well as administer vaccines. If the calf is several days old, the rancher or cowboy might have to rope it with the horse keeping the rope taut while the calf is tended to, just as was done on the range generations ago.

These ranch horses must be roping horses when the need arises; cutting horses when it comes time

Trail riding is growing more popular.

for sorting; speed merchants when a cow breaks from the group and heads for the horizon; and smooth-traveling trail horses when it is time to head home. Unlike their show-ring contemporaries, who perfect a specific skill, the western horses used for today's ranch work must be able to do it all.

These horses come in a variety of sizes and shapes, with varied pedigrees (some are registered). As interest in the western horse and the western way of life continues to grow, a great many western horses are recreational mounts for dude ranches that often cater to city dwellers who dream of riding tall in the saddle along mountain trails. These recreation-oriented ranches offer everything from easy one-hour riding jaunts to week-long pack trips into the mountains.

A number of western ranches offer a western riding and ranching experience for "city slickers" who want to taste the cowboy life. Mounted on staid, safe western horses, guests help gather cattle, sort, and brand. Little does it matter to the "wannabe cowboy" that the same cattle were gathered and sorted a week earlier by another group of city slickers. He or she is on horseback and being a cowboy, and that's all that matters. They head home with tales of their adventures and of making acquaintance with trustworthy western horses. The experience sometimes stimulates them to find a horse of their own, and another fan of the western horse is added to the list.

Countless 4-H programs across the country offer horses as "projects" for young members. Those enrolled learn about proper care and feeding of horses and also have an opportunity to compete for prizes in a wide variety of games and contests. Other western horses are involved in special riding programs for the handicapped.

Still others help patrol American cities as mounts for policemen. Others are used in rescue missions by

A modern cowboy.

special mounted patrols to find lost children, hunters, and hikers in mountain country.

Year after year, the number of western horses in this country continues to grow. However, that interest is not confined to the United States. It is spreading across our borders into other countries, ranging from close neighbors like Canada and Mexico to far away places like Europe, Japan, and Australia.

Quarter Horses are now the most exported western horses, followed by Paints and Appaloosas.

In Canada and Mexico, equine interest is similar to that in the United States where the western horse is popular on the racetrack, as well as in other pursuits.

The foreign market for western horses provides

another outlet for growth. Australia is a good example of how interest in western horses can take hold in other countries.

Australians became interested in the American Quarter Horse in 1954, the year Texas-based King Ranch established its own ranch or station in Australia. The ranch sent some of its top Quarter Horse stallions and broodmares to establish a breeding program "down under." The Australians liked what they saw and began buying Quarter Horses.

In 1964, just ten years after King Ranch arrived, the Australian Quarter Horse Association was formed. Like its American counterpart, it uses the acronym AQHA and is the registry for Australian-bred Quarter Horses. By 2001 some 87,000 Quarter Horses had been registered, and the association boasted a membership of 5,000-plus with 270 affiliates that sponsor Quarter Horse shows. Once a year, the Australian Quarter Horse Championships are held with a full range of halter and performance competition.

The Australian Quarter Horse Association is the second-largest breed registry in the country after the Thoroughbred registry.

Australia raises a great many cattle on huge stations comprising hundreds of thousands of acres. The mentality of these ranchers and their employees is akin to that of ranchers and cowboys in the American West. They want and need western horses that can cover ground, sort, and rope.

In the wake of the King Ranch Quarter Horses, Australians developed a fondness for cutting. Among the

horses King Ranch sent to its Australia division were several that carried the blood of famed cutting horses like Peppy San, Mr. San Peppy, and Peppy San Badger. The cutters struck a responsive chord with the Australians, who began using them extensively in their own breeding programs, as well as in competition.

An event called camp drafting also stimulated Australia's interest in the western horse. Camp drafting combines aspects of team penning and barrel racing, making it a made-to-order contest for the western horse.

Australia represents only a portion of the foreign market. Europeans also have developed a keen interest in the western horse, with Germany, Italy, and France leading the way. Not only are they importing, but they also are establishing breeding programs.

Europe's modern-day infatuation with the western horse can, perhaps, be traced to World War II when the movie industry there went on hiatus, and

An Appaloosa in New Zealand.

imported Westerns filled European screens.

The western lifestyle has continued to fascinate Europeans who, by and large, are importing and breeding western horses that are action or event oriented rather than halter horses. Reining, cutting, and barrel racing, along with western pleasure, are drawing more and more participants.

The Federation Equestre Internationale (FEI) approved reining as an event at the 2002 World Equestrian Games held in Jerez de la Frontera, Spain, in September. Teams from eleven countries participated, with the United States winning the gold medal, Canada the silver, and New Zealand the bronze.

The World Equestrian Games have long been regarded as one of the world's most prestigious equine events. The games bring under one organizational umbrella the world championships for the seven equestrian disciplines governed by the FEI: show jumping, dressage, three-day eventing, carriage driving, endurance racing, vaulting, and now, reining.

The National Reining Horse Association (NRHA) and the AQHA, which worked together to get reining included in the World Equestrian Games, consider this a step toward their ultimate goal of having reining included in the Summer Olympics. The final hurdle to be overcome is approval by a designated Olympic Committee. The AQHA and the NRHA have set a goal of 2012 for the inclusion of reining at the Summer Olympics.

The inclusion of this event at a prestigious gathering such as the World Equestrian Games will open the European market even wider for the western horse.

The World Equestrian Games was a significant event for reining in Europe, but certainly not the first. Each year a NRHA-approved championship is held in Europe. To qualify a team, a participating country must hold two NRHA events during the year. In 2002, reining events were held in countries like Italy, England, Belgium, the Netherlands, Israel, Austria, France, and Germany. Reining competition was also held in Japan.

The western horse is also growing in popularity in the United Kingdom — England, Scotland, and Wales — where English riding competition long has been favored. At the end of 2001, there were 1,616 AQHA-registered Quarter Horses in the United Kingdom. That number is expected to increase.

Barrel racing, long popular in the United States and Australia, has become increasingly global. Italy began barrel racing in earnest in the early 1990s, and other neighboring countries have rapidly adopted the sport as well. In 2001 the National Barrel Horse Association European Championships were held in Reggio Emilia, Italy, just south of Milan. Competing were 110 contestants from Italy, France, Switzerland, and Germany. Each event at the championship sold out.

The U.S. National Barrel Horse Association (NBHA), organized in 1992 and now sporting more than 22,000 members, is pushing for globalization. The goal of the NBHA is to follow in the footsteps of reining and have barrel racing approved both for the World Equestrian Games and the Summer Olympics. The International Barrel Horse Federation has been formed to standardize barrel racing worldwide, educate international newcomers to the sport, and help to establish affiliate associations in foreign countries. To be considered for inclusion in the Olympics, at least twenty countries must participate in the sport. The International Barrel Racing Federation is already well on the way to achieving that goal and has taken aim on the Olympics.

Not all importers, breeders, and owners of western horses in foreign lands are solely interested in competitive action events.

In a country like Brazil, for example, halter horses are very popular. Like some other South American countries, Brazil, which had 1,877 AQHA-registered Quarter Horses at the end of 2001, is a contrast in "haves" and "have-nots" in its population. There is little middle ground. The wealthy are very wealthy and the poor are very poor. Only the wealthy can afford to import and show horses. In many cases, their choice is to have their horses shown at halter, where the owners can garner honor and prestige without being personally involved. Europeans, by contrast, are much more "hands on" and want to ride and compete with their own horses.

Racing is also very popular in Brazil, where some excellent running Quarter Horse and Thoroughbred bloodlines have developed.

When one looks to the Far East, Japan is at the forefront. The country has a thriving Thoroughbred racehorse industry, with the mountainous island of Hokkaido home to many prestigious farms. Through the years, the Japanese have purchased some of the best racehorses possible from the United States, Europe, and Australia. Among those purchases was the celebrated Kentucky Derby winner Sunday Silence.

The Japanese have also been fascinated with the western horse, but their involvement has taken a different turn, which involves riding but not ownership. At the end of the year 2001, there were only 447 AQHA-registered Quarter Horses in Japan. The western horse hasn't experienced the growth in Japan that it has in other places because it's a small land with a huge population. Because the country's lack of space prevents widespread ownership, the Japanese have established dude ranches where they can rent and ride western horses.

International trade of horses has suffered from disease outbreaks. When foot-and-mouth disease erupted in Europe in 2001, many new rules and regulations for animal imports and exports were quickly put into place. Horses were not exempt from the application of stringent regulations even though they do not contract foot-and-mouth disease. Nevertheless, the strict new rules dampened importation and exportation.

However, the setback was temporary. Interest in the western horse continues to grow in Europe and in eastern countries and as a result, so will the market for exported American horses, frozen semen, and perhaps one day, even frozen embryos.

The western horse has traveled a long and exciting trail to arrive at its prominent position in the equine world. The odyssey began with arduous voyages from Spain to Mexico; continued on the dusty plains of the United States where Native Americans harnessed the horse's energies for hunting and war; and fortified when cowboys developed the animal into a valuable companion and helper. There have been bumps in the road. Ranchers viewed the huge herds of wild horses as a curse. Wild horses were captured and slaughtered until they faced extinction before gentler souls stepped in to stop the carnage. Wars killed millions of horses, wiping out entire bloodlines. Through it all, the western horse persevered. Finally, the odyssey has come to rest at a secure destination where the growth and expansion of the western horse is assured by legions of admirers.

Western Horse Resources

American Association of Equine Practitioners
4075 Iron Works Parkway
Lexington, KY 40511
859.233.0147
www.aaep.org

American Buckskin Registry Association
P.O. Box 3850
Redding, CA 96049
530.223.1420
www.americanbuckskin.org

American Paint Horse Association
P.O. Box 961023
Fort Worth, TX 76161-0023
817.834.2742
www.apha.com

American Quarter Horse Association
1600 Quarter Horse Drive
Amarillo, TX 79104
806.376.4811
www.aqha.com

Appaloosa Horse Club
2720 West Pullman Road
Moscow, ID 83843
208.882.5578
www.appaloosa.com

National Barrel Horse Association
725 Broad Street
Augusta, GA 30901-1050
706.722.7223
www.nbha.com

National Cowboy and Western Heritage Museum
1700 NE 63rd Street
Oklahoma City, OK 73111
405.478.2250
www.cowboyhalloffame.org

National Cutting Horse Association
260 Bailey Avenue
Fort Worth, TX 76107-1862
817.244.6188
www.nchacutting.com

National 4-H Council
7100 Connecticut Avenue
Chevy Chase, MD 20815
301.961.2800
www.4-h.org

National High School Rodeo Association
12001 Tejon Street, Suite 128
Denver, CO 80234
800.466.4772
www.nhsra.org

National Reining Horse Association
3000 NW 10th Street
Oklahoma City, OK 73107-5302
405.946.7400
www.nrha.com

National Senior Pro Rodeo Association
1967 North First Street, Suite A
Hamilton, MT 59840
406.375.1400
ww.seniorrodeo.com

Palomino Horse Breeders of America
15253 East Skelly Drive
Tulsa, OK 74116-2637
918.438.1234
www.palominohba.com

Professional Rodeo Cowboys Association
101 ProRodeo Drive
Colorado Springs, CO 80919
719.593.8840
www.prorodeo.com

INDEX

INDEX

INDEX

INDEX

INDEX

Photo Credits

Chapter 1:
Anne M. Eberhardt, pg. 7; Dusty L. Perin, pg. 8

Chapter 2:
Robert E. Cunningham Collection, National Cowboy & Western Heritage Museum, pg. 13, 18; Mark Sullivan, pg. 14, 16

Chapter 3:
Mark Sullivan, pg. 21; Les Sellnow, pg. 23, 25

Chapter 4:
The Blood-Horse, pg. 31; American Quarter Horse Heritage Center and Museum, pg. 33

Chapter 5:
Anne M. Eberhardt, pg. 37, 46 (top right); Dusty L. Perin, pg. 38, 44, 46 (bottom left); Robert E. Cunningham Collection, National Cowboy & Western Heritage Museum, pg. 39; Dickinson Research Center, National Cowboy & Western Heritage Museum, pg. 41

Chapter 6:
Anne M. Eberhardt, pg. 47, 48, 52; Robert E. Cunningham Collection, National Cowboy & Western Heritage Museum, pg. 49, 55; Dusty L. Perin, pg. 51, 56

Chapter 7:
John Brasseaux, pg. 57; American Quarter Horse Heritage Center and Museum, pg. 60, 63, 64, 65

Chapter 8:
Dusty L. Perin, pg. 67, 74 (bottom); American Paint Horse Association, pg. 72; John Brasseaux, pg. 74 (top)

Chapter 9:
Dusty L. Perin, pg. 79; Robert E. Cunningham Collection, National Cowboy & Western Heritage Museum, pg. 81; Hugh Miller, pg. 83; Signal Corps, pg. 84

Chapter 10:
John Brasseaux, pg. 86, 92; American Quarter Horse Heritage Center and Museum, pg. 88, 89, 90

Chapter 11:
Anne M. Eberhardt, pg. 95, 97, 98, 99, 100; Dusty L. Perin, pg. 101

Chapter 12:
Courtesy of the Tom Mix Collection, Oklahoma Historical Society, pg. 106; Courtesy of Autry Qualified Interest Trust, pg. 107; Courtesy of the Roy Rogers-Dale Evans Museum, pg. 108

Chapter 13:
John Brasseaux, pg. 112, 116, 117; W. Dickinson, pg. 113

Chapter 14:
Anne M. Eberhardt, pg. 120, 121; Dusty L. Perin, pg. 122

Back Cover:
Robert E. Cunningham Collection, National Cowboy & Western Heritage Museum; American Quarter Horse Heritage Center and Museum; John Brasseaux

About The Author

Les Sellnow

Les Sellnow has been a lifelong journalist and horseman. He has competed in a variety of equine disciplines, ranging from combined training to cutting and from endurance racing to western and English pleasure.

Earlier in his career Sellnow owned and operated a training stable in Minnesota, with emphasis on preparing young horses for riding and driving careers. As a journalist he spent twenty-two years with the Brainerd (Minnesota) *Daily Dispatch*, rising from reporter to editor, winning state and national writing awards along the way.

He and his wife, Linda, moved from Minnesota to Kentucky in 1984, where he served as editor of *National Show Horse* magazine and was a free-lance writer for *The Blood-Horse* magazine. In 1994 the Sellnows moved to a ranch in the Wind River Valley near Riverton, Wyoming.

Sellnow is a regular contributor to *The Horse: Your Guide to Equine Health Care* magazine and has had both fiction and non-fiction books published, including *Understanding Equine Lameness* and *Understanding the Young Horse*, part of The Horse Health Care Library published by Eclipse Press.

OTHER TITLES FROM ECLIPSE PRESS

THOROUGHBRED Legends® SERIES

ECLIPSE PRESS

A Division of Blood-Horse Publications
PUBLISHERS SINCE 1916